Cambridge Elements

Elements in the Philosophy of Ludwig Wittgenstein
edited by
David G. Stern
University of Iowa

WITTGENSTEIN ON PRIVATE LANGUAGE, SENSATION AND PERCEPTION

Michael Hymers
Dalhousie University

Shaftesbury Road, Cambridge CB2 8EA, United Kingdom

One Liberty Plaza, 20th Floor, New York, NY 10006, USA

477 Williamstown Road, Port Melbourne, VIC 3207, Australia

314–321, 3rd Floor, Plot 3, Splendor Forum, Jasola District Centre, New Delhi – 110025, India

103 Penang Road, #05–06/07, Visioncrest Commercial, Singapore 238467

Cambridge University Press is part of Cambridge University Press & Assessment, a department of the University of Cambridge.

We share the University's mission to contribute to society through the pursuit of education, learning and research at the highest international levels of excellence.

www.cambridge.org
Information on this title: www.cambridge.org/9781009506793

DOI: 10.1017/9781108946551

© Michael Hymers 2025

This publication is in copyright. Subject to statutory exception and to the provisions of relevant collective licensing agreements, no reproduction of any part may take place without the written permission of Cambridge University Press & Assessment.

When citing this work, please include a reference to the DOI 10.1017/9781108946551

First published 2025

A catalogue record for this publication is available from the British Library

ISBN 978-1-009-50679-3 Hardback
ISBN 978-1-108-93117-5 Paperback
ISSN 2632-7112 (online)
ISSN 2632-7104 (print)

Cambridge University Press & Assessment has no responsibility for the persistence or accuracy of URLs for external or third-party internet websites referred to in this publication and does not guarantee that any content on such websites is, or will remain, accurate or appropriate.

For EU product safety concerns, contact us at Calle de José Abascal, 56, 1°, 28003 Madrid, Spain, or email eugpsr@cambridge.org

Wittgenstein on Private Language, Sensation and Perception

Elements in the Philosophy of Ludwig Wittgenstein

DOI: 10.1017/9781108946551
First published online: September 2025

Michael Hymers
Dalhousie University
Author for correspondence: Michael Hymers, michael.hymers@dal.ca

Abstract: Wittgenstein's critique of private language in the *Philosophical Investigations* does not attempt to refute the possibility of a private sensation-language, let alone in any *one* argument, as has often been thought. Nor does it aim to establish that language is intrinsically social. Instead, PI §§ 243–315 present a series of arguments, suggestions, questions, examples and thought-experiments whose purpose is to undermine the temptation to think of sensations and perceptual experiences as private objects occupying a private phenomenal space. These themes are clear developments of Wittgenstein's earlier critique of sense-datum theories (1929–1936) and his insight that naming is more complex than he had assumed in the *Tractatus*.

Keywords: Wittgenstein, private language, sensation, phenomenal space, object-and-name model

© Michael Hymers 2025

ISBNs: 9781009506793 (HB), 9781108931175 (PB), 9781108946551 (OC)
ISSNs: 2632-7112 (online), 2632-7104 (print)

Contents

1 Introduction   1

2 Methodological and Exegetical Commitments   4

3 Privacy and the Objectification of Sensation and Perception   8

4 Private Language   12

5 Solitary Speakers   15

6 Ontological Privacy, Epistemic Privacy and First-Person Authority   18

7 Avowals   25

8 The First Wave: Verification and Memory   28

9 The Second Wave: Ostensive Definition   31

10 The Third Wave: Rules   34

11 The Fourth Wave: Stage-Setting   38

12 The Human Manometer   45

13 The Beetle   56

14 Epilogue   63

List of Abbreviations of the Works Cited   64

References   66

1 Introduction

This Element examines Wittgenstein's views on sensation, perception and private language at §§243–315 of the *Philosophical Investigations*, drawing on *The Big Typescript* and Wittgenstein's lectures and notes beginning in 1929. Wittgenstein is widely credited with producing the 'Private Language Argument,' which ostensibly tries to show that a private language is logically impossible. This is often taken to mean that, if the argument works, language logically presupposes a community of speakers. It is not just paradigmatically, but *essentially,* social.

What the argument is and whether it succeeds are contentious, but a long-standing consensus locates it at PI §258. Here Wittgenstein imagines keeping a private diary of one's sensations, designated by terms defined by fixing one's attention on one's sensations and associating names with them. Supposedly, Wittgenstein argues that this procedure *must* fail, either because the connection between term 'S' and sensation S cannot be remembered later or because no connection has been established. An influential dissenting view purports to find the Private Language Argument earlier in the *Investigations* in the discussion of rule-following: if rule-following is essentially social, then so is language.

I argue, to the contrary, that Wittgenstein's critique of private language neither reduces to a single argument nor attempts a definitive refutation. Rather, we find an array of arguments and examples designed to show that a certain way of thinking about sensation and perception – as objects situated in phenomenal space – is not obligatory, at best, and has been given no clear content, at worst. Wittgenstein thus advances no general thesis about the nature of language (e.g., that it is intrinsically social).

In Section 2, I connect these claims to some general considerations about Wittgenstein's philosophical method, arguing that his remarks on philosophy at PI §§89–133 should be understood not as aiming to do away, once and for all, with all philosophical problems but as reimagining the ongoing task of philosophy as alleviating particular philosophical confusions, as they arise, by attending to overlooked aspects of the grammar of the terms in which those confusions are expressed.

Section 3 traces concerns about the object-model of sensation and perceptual appearances to Wittgenstein's critique of sense-datum theories, from 1929 through his lectures of the mid-1930s. Here he criticises our tendency to model visual space or tactual space on physical space and to think of sensations and perceptions as objects – sense-data – occupying these phenomenal spaces. Because my phenomenal space does not overlap with yours, my sensations seem to be *private* objects that no one else can have or know directly. However, physical space is a dubious model for phenomenal space, and it is unclear how I could *own* something that no one else could. Wittgenstein's complaints with private *language* derive from these concerns, together with his realisation that naming is more complex than supposed in the *Tractatus*: the resources available for naming in public language are stripped away by the very hypothesis that I might learn the meanings of sensation-terms from acquaintance with my own sensations. It is thus puzzling how a private sensation-language could get started.

These considerations cast doubt on the suggestion (Section 5) that Wittgenstein is targeting the language of a solitary speaker. Rather, his critical target is a language whose terms would get their meanings from sensations construed as private objects. I further distinguish (Section 4) the 'ordinary' privacy of our sensations from their alleged 'superprivacy' (NPL, 447) and their epistemic privacy from their ontological privacy, turning (Section 6) to a discussion of first-person authority – our acknowledged entitlement to express our own experiences. Were sensations phenomenal objects, this authority might derive from our privileged access to the private objects of our experience. However, we could as plausibly see it as a grammatical characteristic of paradigmatic first-person uses of verbs of experience, which are analogous to non-verbal expressions (Sections 6 and 7).

In Sections 8–11, I distinguish four 'waves' of interpretation that have washed over the *Investigations* since 1953, carving channels through which much subsequent reading flows. A recurrent theme of the first three waves is the assumption noted earlier that Wittgenstein has a central argument – *the* Private Language Argument, often located in the diary-example – which aims to refute the logical possibility of a private language.

The First Wave (Section 8) presents this fabled refutation as a verificationist challenge to the private speaker's ability to remember how to apply the terms of a private language. Such readings sometimes flirt with behaviourism or collapse the distinction between private language and solitary language. They also attribute to Wittgenstein a problematic theory of meaning and reduce the refutation to scepticism about memory.

The Second Wave (Section 9) remains preoccupied with the diary-example but correctly bypasses epistemic considerations for semantic ones. Wittgenstein's real concern is not whether the private diarist could *remember* the correct use of a private sensation-term, but whether the term could be *defined* in the first place.

These considerations, however, are swamped by the Third Wave (Section 10), which seeks 'the real "private language argument"' (Kripke 1982, 3) in Wittgenstein's discussion of rule-following (PI §§185–242). On this reading, Wittgenstein is a sceptic about rule-following, who holds that we can be justified (but never *right*) in attributing understanding to others, only if our community would agree. This view collapses the distinction between private language and solitary language, and it ignores the provenance of Wittgenstein's discussion of privacy in his transitional writings.

The Fourth Wave (Section 11) takes many forms but is generally driven by a re-evaluation of Wittgenstein's work as a whole. For my purposes, it matters most for rescuing the insights of the Second Wave, for eroding the idea of 'The Private Language Argument,' and for drawing attention to the origins of Wittgenstein's discussion of privacy and private language in his transitional writings.

At PI §270 the diary-example of PI §258 is modified by the suggestion that I might use a manometer to discover a correlation between the sensation S and an increase in my blood-pressure. I endorse Hacker's claim (Section 12) that this example is meant to undermine the idea that the meanings of sensation-terms rest on the (re)identification of sensations, as they would if sensations were like objects. However, I argue that the example is usefully read through the prism of Wittgenstein's treatment of the inverted spectrum (PI §272) – the old idea that there might be undetectable differences in the ways you and I see colours. Wittgenstein argues that this seems possible only if we sever attributions of colour-perception from the behavioural criteria on which they ordinarily rest. Doing so reduces perceptions to superprivate objects with no bearing on the uses of colour-terms. It cannot, then, matter whether we correctly identify those objects or not.

Finally (Section 13), I examine the much-discussed beetle in a box of PI §293, which compares the idea that I might learn the meaning of 'pain' from my own sensation to the idea that everyone might own a box containing something called a 'beetle,' which no one else can see. This is the *Investigations*' most explicit expression of doubt about the 'object-and-name' model of sensation-language encouraged by the misleading metaphor of phenomenal space. Misunderstandings of this passage have provoked worries about behaviourism, but such worries themselves *presuppose* the object-and-name model.

No topic in Wittgenstein's philosophy has generated as much commentary and as little consensus – about understanding Wittgenstein and about whether he is correct – as the discussion of private language. Over 40 years ago, Stewart Candlish joked that 'no one with a concern for his own health' (1980, 85) would try to master the huge secondary literature on this topic. The challenge has only grown, but I have tried to acknowledge as much of the extensive commentary as I can. I have overlooked some items for pragmatic reasons, and I am sure to have neglected others through inattention or forgetfulness. I beg my readers' indulgence.

2 Methodological and Exegetical Commitments

At PI §§89–133[1] Wittgenstein suggests that the philosopher's task is not to give explanations resembling scientific hypotheses (PI §§109, 126) about the fundamental nature of language or meaning or mind but to clarify such concepts (PI §§109, 118–119, 122, 125, 133) by revealing overlooked aspects of the grammar of the language in which we formulate them (PI §§122, 129–133). Philosophical puzzlement often arises when we are misled by 'certain analogies between the forms of expression in different regions of our language' (PI §90), and overcoming that puzzlement demands '*an overview* of the use of our words' (PI §122). We need '*complete* clarity. But this simply means that the philosophical problems should *completely* disappear' (PI §133).

The interpretation of these and related remarks is controversial and has become a central concern for readers since what I call later (Section 11) the 'Fourth Wave.' According to Robert Fogelin, they express a 'neo-Pyrrhonian' impulse 'to eliminate philosophy altogether' (1994, 205).[2] This impulse struggles with a 'non-Pyrrhonian' one, which seeks 'to *replace* his earlier foundationalist theory with a nonfoundationalist theory' (205). Pyrrhonian and non-Pyrrhonian interpretations of the text, accordingly, emphasise one impulse over the other.[3]

Fogelin leaves no room for the thought that Wittgenstein wants to forsake 'traditional philosophy in order to do philosophy better' (Stern 2004, 35) *without* simply offering another theory. An analogy from 1931 suggests such a possibility. Wittgenstein compares philosophy to an infinite strip that may be divided into problems, either lengthwise or crosswise. Traditional philosophy tries 'to grasp the unlimited strips,' and it seems 'that it cannot be done piecemeal':

> To be sure it cannot, if by a piece one means an infinite longitudinal strip. But it may well be done, if one means a cross-strip. – But in that case we never get to the end of our work! – Of course not, for it has no end. (Z §447)

The task of philosophy is ongoing, but philosophy does not grapple with timeless problems (infinite strips). Rather, its problems are continually produced and reproduced by the structure of our language (PI §115):

> So long as there is a verb 'be' that seems to function like 'eat' and 'drink', so long as there are the adjectives 'identical', 'true', 'false', 'possible', so long as there is talk about a flow of time and an expanse of space, etc., etc., humans will continue to bump up against the same mysterious difficulties, and stare at something that no explanation seems able to remove. (BT 424)

---

[1] See BT 406–435. [2] For worries about the comparison to Pyrrhonism, see Marion 2022.
[3] For more, see Fogelin 1994, 205–220 and Stern 2004, 34–38, 46–55.

These problems owe their longevity to the structure of European languages. This does not make them eternal or universal. A language with a sufficiently different structure, we could conjecture, might have different philosophical preoccupations. But, for those embedded in a particular tradition, the task of the philosopher must be 'to put up signs to help in getting past the dangerous spots' (BT 423) – those places in the language where we are tempted by misleading grammatical analogies, for example.

The finite cross-strips of Wittgenstein's analogy are particular grammatical confusions that must be dealt with one at a time: 'Problems are solved (difficulties eliminated) but not a *single* problem' (PI §133). Further difficulties always remain. Our language is complex. The task of getting a synoptic view of our grammar is multifaceted. The 'ancient city' of language is ever-expanding with 'new suburbs' (PI §18) for us to get lost in. (Consider the philosophical puzzles produced by the advent of the digital computer.) It should be unsurprising that the philosopher's work has no end.

But what is that work like? Peter Hacker, a careful reader of Wittgenstein's remarks on method (Baker and Hacker 2005 [1983], 251–334), takes them to eschew theory-building and explanation in favour of describing grammatical rules and showing that traditional philosophy *violates* them – 'that certain suppositions, certain putative doctrines, *make no sense*' (287). The discussion of private language, then, tries to show that 'the idea of a private language that is implicitly invoked by so many philosophical doctrines is . . . incoherent' (287).

Interpreters like Stephen Mulhall complain, however, that, even if Hacker's reading does not commit Wittgenstein to an alternative theory, in aiming to demonstrate that talk of private language is literally 'nonsensical or incoherent, a violation of grammar' (Mulhall 2007, 18), it remains 'substantial' (18) in a way that goes beyond Wittgenstein's intentions. By contrast, Mulhall's 'resolute' (18) reading sees Wittgenstein as imagining various things an interlocutor might mean by 'private language' but failing to find anything that will satisfy the interlocutor (18–19), leaving it open that there might yet be some meaningful construal of the interlocutor's words.

Gordon Baker, having earlier collaborated with Hacker, similarly repudiates the substantial approach, suggesting that Wittgenstein seeks to draw our attention to neglected aspects of our grammar, not to patrol 'the bounds of sense, sharply reprimanding philosophers who commit offences by uttering nonsense' (2004, 94). Wittgenstein's goal is therapeutic in a way analogous to the 'treatment of a particular patient rather than [to] a kind of campaign to improve public health' (132). It is particular, not general, in its aims, and it 'propos[es] other ways of seeing things' (290), not demonstrations of the incoherence of views under criticism.

I can make no significant contribution to these debates here. I can only try to situate my own approach. Like Hacker, I doubt that Wittgenstein is best read as seeking to end philosophy once and for all. The work of his philosophy, however, is pursued not by replacing old theories with better ones, nor by showing extant views to be nonsense. The point of acquiring a 'surveyable representation' (PI §122) of the grammar of the expressions that puzzle us, I contend, is to help us to see 'connections' (BT 417) we have overlooked – for example, between the grammar of sensation-terms and the grammar of colour-terms (Sections 3 and 6.1) – in much the way that noticing a visual aspect consists in seeing an 'internal relation' (PPF xi §247) between, for example, the duck-rabbit and other images of rabbits. So, like Baker (2004), I think that drawing attention to overlooked aspects of our grammar is central to Wittgenstein's approach.[4]

There may be more than one connection to emphasise: 'We want to establish an order in our knowledge of the use of language: an order for a particular purpose, one out of many possible orders, not *the* order' (PI §132). So, again, like Baker (2004) and Mulhall (2007, 18), I do not think that Wittgenstein's goal in the private-language discussion is to show the idea of a private language to be nonsense because it violates *the* rules of grammar. This much already follows from a conception of grammar present in 1930:

> It cannot be proved that it is nonsense to say of a colour that it is a semitone higher than another. I can only say 'If anyone uses words with the meanings that I do, then he can connect no sense with this combination. If it makes sense to him, he must understand something different by these words from what I do.' (PR §4)

It may seem that, on my reading, Wittgenstein really *is* trying to refute the possibility of a private language because I emphasise an array of *arguments* with their roots in Wittgenstein's reflections from 1929 onward. However, these arguments are best read as trying to show that certain received views about sensation and perception are *not obviously correct* – that we can look at the grammar of sensation and perception in another way, and that defenders of private language have not *yet* given clear content to their proposals (though I hope it will also be clear that Wittgenstein leaves these defenders little cause for *optimism*). Moreover, the arguments *are* part of the text, and much light is cast on Wittgenstein's discussion by making them explicit.

These remarks are compatible with acknowledging that the *Investigations* is not written in a univocal voice – that the impulses to provide a better theory or to show that talk of private language is nonsense or to do away with philosophy

---

[4] The concern appears as early as 1930 (Hymers 2021, 79–81).

completely all find expression in the complex dialogical structure of the book. 'What we are "tempted to say",' in these cases, ' ... is, of course, not philosophy; but it is its raw material' (PI §254). There are, as David Stern argues (2004, 21–28), many voices in the *Investigations*, and it is difficult and contentious to identify any of them with *the* voice of the author. We do not suppose, however, that Ravel's voice, in his 1914 *Trio in A minor*, is really the piano, not the violin or cello, and we need not see Yuri as merely the mouthpiece of Pasternak to find a critique of the Bolshevik revolution in *Doctor Zhivago*. I read the *Investigations* in a similar spirit – as a mature expression of arguments Wittgenstein had formulated (sometimes much earlier), which attempts to exemplify the attraction of the problems with which it deals, presenting them as the raw material of philosophy, and then showing that these problems are not inevitable.

I advance several claims informed by these thoughts. First, 'there is no such thing as "the private language argument"' (Canfield 2001, 378). Rather, we find a collection of arguments, questions, thought-experiments and so on, whose goal is to break the grip that a certain way of thinking about sensation and perception has on us in reflective moments. There is neither one central argument, nor one that aims to defeat all comers.[5]

Relatedly, Wittgenstein advances no general thesis about the nature of language in these remarks: he does not argue that language is intrinsically social. He seeks to avoid puzzlement produced, particularly, by a misleading analogy between physical space and phenomenal space – the space(s) of sensation and perception – and to remind us of the extensive resources on which we ordinarily rely when naming something in public language. The analogy invites us to objectify our sensations and perceptions and to expect the properties of the resulting 'objects' to mimic the properties of physical objects – to expect these 'objects' to be persistent, divisible, recurrent, reidentifiable and so on. The fact that my phenomenal space does not overlap with yours then makes it tempting to suppose that I have exclusive ownership and exclusive knowledge of my sense-data. However, the more we emphasise the privacy of these objects, the more we undermine the analogy that invited us to think about them, for we have stripped away what we presuppose in our everyday applications of language, and it becomes puzzling how we could ever name such private objects.

Critics may complain that I rely too much on statements of Wittgenstein's method from the early 1930s and that the arguments I take as basic to the discussion of privacy are similarly dated. Others will protest that I understate

---

[5] See also Baker 2004, 125–127. For similar points see, e.g., Cook 1972, 46; Cooke 1974; Cavell 1979, 344; Stroud 2002 [1983], 69; Stern 2004, 171–185; Mulhall 2007, 99; Fogelin 2009, 56–78; Horwich 2012, 197–198.

what has been achieved by the *Investigations* – that the arguments clearly refute the privacy of sensation and the possibility of a private language.

So perhaps I will satisfy no one, but many passages on method in the *Investigations* survive from the *Big Typescript* and harmonise with my reading, and the early arguments against privacy and private language are also clearly present. A proper appreciation of the text must at least make these arguments explicit, and doing so brings into focus the great coherence of PI §§243–315. At the same time, Wittgenstein's remarks on method suggest that these arguments do not aim at categorical refutations but at helping us recognise overlooked aspects of our grammar, so that what seemed like inevitable features of sensation and perception begin to look like contingent features of our ways of describing them (PI § 104).

3 Privacy and the Objectification of Sensation and Perception

Wittgenstein's discussion of private language does not aim to demonstrate anything about the nature of language as such, but it does invite us to reconsider the grammar of our terminology for sensation and perception: it invites us not to model such terminology on names for spatio-temporal objects. This point has been frequently recognised,[6] but its central importance emerges from Wittgenstein's writings of 1929 to the mid-1930s.

Wittgenstein here first challenges both the object-model of sensations and perceptual appearances and the privacy of sensations and perceptual appearances. His criticisms, beginning in 1929, have two interrelated targets: the misleading analogy between physical space and phenomenal space, and sense-datum theories of perception. The latter target may be surprising. In his 1930–32 Cambridge lectures (LWL) Wittgenstein mentions sense-data frequently and uncritically. However, though he adopts the Cambridge vernacular for his students, his concurrent manuscripts repeatedly criticise sense-datum theories, most notably for their commitment to private objects. I begin with sense-datum theories and then turn to phenomenal space.

When G. E. Moore revived the term 'sense-data' (Moore 1909–10, 57), he emphasised the 'act-object' analysis of sensation and perception, for which he had argued in 1903. On this analysis, we must distinguish the act of perception

---

[6] E.g., Malcolm 1954, 540, 556–557; Pole 1958, 63–78; Cook 1965, 302, 305–306, 311–313; Pears 1971, 143; Hacker 1972, 246–248; Kenny 1973, 181–182; Cooke 1974, 32; Hopkins 1974, 122; Senchuk 1976, 222; Finch 1977, 127–146; Williams 1983, 59, 71; Sauvé 1985, 10; Gert 1986, 413; Fogelin 1987, 169–170; Pears 1988, 416–417; Budd 1989, 48–68; Hanfling 1989, 89–90, 93–95; Tugendhat 1986, 97; Canfield 2001, 379–380; Baker 2004, 126; Schroeder 2006, 182–185, 201–207, 219; Nielsen 2008, 50; Schulte 2011, 445–446; Sluga 2011, 73; McDougall 2013, 44–46, 61–65; Schroeder 2013, 201; Hacker 2019a [1990], 17–23.

or sensation from its object. Otherwise, like Berkeley, we may confuse sensation or perception as an *act* with sensation or perception as an *object* and infer that the objects of sensation and perception are *ideas* because the acts of sensation and perception are mental (1903, 445–446). In 1909–10 Moore identified the *immediate* objects of sensation and perception as sense-data, and the *mediate* objects of sensation and perception as spatio-temporal objects, but he left unsettled whether sense-data were *representations* of spatio-temporal objects (representational realism), *constitutive* of spatio-temporal objects (phenomenalism), or identical with parts of surfaces of spatio-temporal objects (naïve realism). The first two answers treat sense-data as private objects.

Wittgenstein's complaints with sense-data, beginning in October 1929, were various, but two matter here: that sense-data cannot be *privately owned*, and that sensations and perceptual appearances are not *objects*. Consider privacy.

> In the sense of the phrase 'sense data' in which it is inconceivable that someone else should have them, it cannot, for this very reason, be said that someone else does not have them. And by the same token, it's senseless to say that *I*, as opposed to someone else, *have* them. (PR §61; BT 510)

The manuscript version of this passage (29 November 1929) continues: 'This simply shows that something is not in order with the concept of sense-data' (MS 107, 216). A year later he returns to the argument: 'What is essentially private, or seems that way, doesn't have an owner' (BT 508). If no one else can have my sensations, then there is no sense in saying that *I* have them. Ownership implies that another might own them, as someone else will own my house if I sell it.

It is not just the private *ownership* of sensations that bothers Wittgenstein:

> What is this supposed to mean: He has *these* pains? Unless it is supposed to mean that he has *such* pains: i.e. pains of such intensity, kind, etc. But only in that sense can I too have 'these pains'.
> That means that the subject-object form is not applicable to this. (BT 508)

The idea that I might *own* my sensations suggests that they are *objects* (as sense-datum theories propose). But we might as plausibly see pains as *qualities*, not objects, 'and if they coincide in intensity, etc., etc., then they are the same; just as two suits are the *same* colour if they correspond with respect to brightness, saturation, etc.' (BT 510; PR §61; cf. BBB 55; RSD, 292–293). Moreover, objects occupy space: they are 'around' the body and 'have an effect on it' (BT 508). But the 'space' of sensation is not like this, as becomes evident when we 'examine what sort of facts we call criteria for a pain being in a certain place' (BBB 49).

Ordinarily, if I feel pain in one hand, I can locate it with my other hand. I feel my right hand palpating my left until the tender spot is reached, and I *see* the movements of my right hand. Perhaps this convergence of visual, tactile and kinaesthetic indicators encourages us to think of sensations as objects – it resembles their convergence in the case of objects in physical space. When these indicators of physical objects *diverge* – when I seem to see something but cannot touch it – I suspect an illusion.

No such failure of convergence may seem imaginable for sensation. However, the convergence is an empirical regularity, not a metaphysical necessity. 'The man whose foot has been amputated will describe a particular pain as pain in his foot' (BBB 52; cf. BT 514), but this location in pain space has no correlate in tactual or kinaesthetic space. Probing with my finger will not isolate the pain in my severed foot, and this location of the pain corresponds to nothing in visual space or physical space. Stranger cases are possible:

> Thus we can imagine a person having the sensation of toothache plus those tactual and kinaesthetic experiences which are normally bound up with seeing his hand travelling from *his* tooth to his nose, to his eyes, etc., but correlated to the visual experience of his hand moving to those places in another person's face. (BBB 52)

This would amount to feeling 'toothache in another person's tooth' (BBB 53). The grammar of sensation-talk is thus unlike the grammar of object-talk, despite the 'apparent analogy' (BBB 49) between them, and recognising the disanalogies between physical space and the spaces of sensation (tactile, kinaesthetic, pain-) dulls the temptation to think of sensations as objects.

A related examination (BT 514) can be made of the misleading analogy between physical space and visual space. Visual space in some ways resembles space proper. Things in my visual field appear to the right or left, above or below, before or behind others. However, pushed further, the analogy collapses. *I* do not exist in visual space (PI §399), so nothing is behind me (BT 461) or at any determinate distance from me (BT 439) in visual space. I can stand across from a table but not 'across from my optical after-image of the table' (BT 439). In physical space, the relation of being the same length is transitive: if marks A and B are the same length, and marks B and C are the same length, then A and C are also the same length, and I can measure two things against a common standard. In visual space, marks A and B may appear the same length, as may marks B and C, but it does not follow that A and C will appear the same length. How they *appear* to me is just how they *are* in visual space, so they are not the same length in visual space (BT 446–447, 453–454; PR §215), and there can be no measurement of them (PR §212).[7]

---

[7] For more see Hymers 2017, 6–23, 32–59.

Overlooking these aspects of the 'grammar' of visual space, I may think that perceiving material objects consists in immediately apprehending phenomenal objects – sense-data. I may reason, 'if something seems to be red, then *something* must have *been* red' (BT 489) – an inference Wittgenstein later describes as the 'objectification' of appearances, in which '[w]e assimilate the grammar of appearance to the grammar of physical objects' (RSD 312). About those phenomenal objects I will want to draw inferences like those I draw about physical objects: that they can be divided (BT 449–452; PR §139), clearly distinguished from each other, re-identified later – that I can give them *names*. Similarly, if I objectify my sensations, it will be easy to suppose that I 'can point to the pain, as it were unseen by the other person, and name it' (LPE 206).

Wittgenstein emphasises the alleged ontological privacy of sensation and perception, their 'privacy of ownership', but he sees this as entailing their 'epistemic privacy' (Hacker 1972, 222).[8] ' ... I alone can know that I am feeling pain, etc.' (PG 129/BT 95 r) if these happenings are private. So a successful critique of the ontological privacy of sensation and perception removes the strongest reason for accepting their epistemic privacy.

These complaints with the privacy of sensation and perception predate Wittgenstein's explicit complaints with private *language*, but they quickly follow his rejection of the idea of a 'phenomenological' or 'primary language' (PR §1), which he entertained in 1929. Such a language would capture immediate experience, in contrast to a secondary or 'physical language' (PR §68), which would talk about the world. The idea of a phenomenological language was to answer Frank Ramsey's criticisms of the *Tractatus*. Wittgenstein had contended that all sentences of natural language could be analysed into logically independent, elementary propositions about simple objects. Ramsey observed (1923, 473–474) that the logical independence of such propositions was incompatible with Wittgenstein's contention that the only necessary statements were tautologies (TLP 6.37). That it is impossible '[f]or two colours, *e.g.*, to be at one place in the visual field' (TLP 6.3751) does not *look* like a tautology, nor is it obvious how to transform it into one.

In response, Wittgenstein tried to redefine 'tautology' and imagined a language whose elementary propositions would assign Cartesian coordinates to patches of colour in the visual field (RLF, 31–32), but he soon worried that doing so amounted to treating these patches as phenomenal objects (MS 105, 11/13; 106, 153) – sense-data. This, he decided, was 'nonsense' (MS 105, 29). He makes no *explicit* suggestion that such objects would be private, but they

---

[8] For this distinction see also Malcolm 1967, 129; Kenny 1973, 186; Vohra 1976, 509; Hallett 1977, 325; Glock 1996, 304–309; Hacker 2019a [1990], 25–68.

supposedly belong to immediate experience, and Wittgenstein's attacks on sense-data begin (MS 107, 171) *days* before he renounces the project of constructing a phenomenological language (MS 107, 176).

Additionally, his critique of private objects and phenomenal space suggests a complaint against private *language*. If we think of sensations and perceptual appearances as objects, it will seem that we can name them and speak of them, as we do public objects, even if they are supposed private. However, we thereby underestimate the resources needed to name even a public object – resources unavailable in the private case. The *Tractatus* had taken the meaning of a name to be its bearer (TLP 3.203), but by 1931 Wittgenstein concluded that pointing at an object could not by itself determine the meaning of a name:

> The name I give to an object, a surface, a place, a colour, has a different grammar in each of these cases. 'A' in 'A is yellow' has a different grammar when it is the name of an object from when it is the name of the surface of an object ...
> And a person who points to an object thereby points to its colour, its shape, the place where it is; but for that very reason he is pointing to it in a different sense in each case. (BT 33)

Pointing requires disambiguation if a name is to be defined. This can be done in language by specifying whether we are defining the name of an object, a colour, a shape, a location, a number, and so on. For someone learning the rudiments of a language (BT 31 v), however, all these concepts must themselves first be learned before ostensive definition is possible.

What holds for ordinary public language we should expect for a private language, too. Thus, if we try to imagine a child-genius who 'invents a name for the pain *himself* even though he wasn't taught one,' we forget 'that all sorts of things in the language have to have been prepared in advance ... for the mere act of naming to make sense' (BT 209 v).

This argument from 1934 reappears at PI §257 (see Section 11), and appreciating it is essential to understanding Wittgenstein's critique of private language in the *Investigations*. Wittgenstein's doubts about the 'object and name' (PI §293) model of sensation-vocabulary are of central importance to his arguments in the *Investigations*, and those doubts are rooted in his criticisms of the metaphor of phenomenal space, which encourages the objectification of sensation and perceptual experience. These assumptions guide my discussion.

4 Private Language

Meaning in a private language – if the idea can be made intelligible – inherits its privacy from the alleged privacy of sensations and perceptual appearances.

'Private language' is thus not a general category for Wittgenstein, of which sensation-language (conceived a certain way) is an instance. These points often eluded early readers.

From about 1954 to 1972 the 'First Wave' of interpreters of the *Philosophical Investigations*, who faced a daunting task, were often puzzled about private language. Was it the language of a solitary speaker isolated from birth (Ayer 1954, 70)?[9] –A code that no one ever deciphers? –A language that describes or names one's sensations (Strawson 1954, 84)?[10] –A sensation-language the learning of which depends on knowing no other language (Todd 1962, 206)?

Confusion surrounded the term 'language'. Might Wittgenstein's view entail the 'absurd demand' that a private language 'have no regularities whatsoever, either of usages or constructions' (Hervey 1957, 71)? Surely, to assume such a lack of rules of use and syntax would be to give 'an unfair *reductio ad absurdum*' (Castañeda 1962, 96)![11]

However, this preoccupation with syntax and vocabulary,[12] because it assumes that sensations and appearances are private objects to which we can refer unproblematically, misses the fundamental lesson that the very idea of a private language remains unclear. Wittgenstein wonders whether a clear story can be told about even the *rudiments* of a private language.

Early puzzlement about language was encouraged by puzzlement about *privacy*. Thus, P. F. Strawson contends that a private vocabulary might equally 'stand ... for things like colours or material objects or animals' not just for 'the sensations of the user of the language' (1954, 84).[13] A. J. Ayer correctly distinguishes a language that is 'necessarily private' because 'used by some particular person to refer only to his private experiences' (1954, 64) from a contingently private language, 'intelligible only to a single person, or to a restricted set of people' (63). However, he then argues that a 'Robinson Crusoe', raised by wolves, could invent a necessarily private language *because* he could invent a *solitary* language to name and describe things on his island (70).

Wittgenstein himself distinguishes contingent privacy from necessary privacy:

> A human being can encourage himself, give himself orders, obey, blame and punish himself; he can ask himself a question and answer it. So one could

---

[9] See also Hervey 1957, 70–71; Tanburn 1963.
[10] See also Hardin 1959, 521; Wellman 1962, 446.
[11] Cf. Todd 1962, 206; Ziedins 1966; Haque 1984.
[12] Something like it persists in the sympathetic suggestion that Wittgenstein tries to show that a 'family' of sentences will not be truth-apt if 'the "seems right"/ "is right" distinction can [not] be made good for them' (Wright 2001, 244).
[13] See also Ambrose 1954, 115.

> imagine human beings who spoke only in monologue, who accompanied their activities by talking to themselves. – An explorer who watched them and listened to their talk might succeed in translating their language into ours. (This would enable him to predict these people's actions correctly, for he also hears them making resolutions and decisions.)
>
> But is it also conceivable that there be a language in which a person could write down or give voice to his inner experiences – his feelings, moods, and so on – for his own use? – – Well, can't we do so in our ordinary language? – But that is not what I mean. The words of this language are to refer to what only the speaker can know – to his immediate private sensations. So another person cannot understand the language. (PI §243)

Asking myself a question or keeping a coded diary involves 'contingent' or 'ordinary' privacy, whether because others do not hear my question or because they happen not to understand my code. A language that others cannot understand because its terms refer to things of which they can have no experience or knowledge involves 'necessary' or 'logical' privacy. In his 'Notes for the "Philosophical Lecture"' (c.1942), Wittgenstein calls it 'superprivacy' (NPL, 447), and *this* is the clear target of his criticisms.

These criticisms readily allow the occasional, ordinary, epistemic privacy of our sensations:[14] I can sometimes conceal my sensations from you. Moreover, *my* sensations are the ones that *I* feel, the ones to which *I* give expression. Such facts, Wittgenstein suggests, belong to the *grammar* of sensation-vocabulary: 'The sentence "Sensations are private" is comparable to "One plays patience by oneself"' (PI §248). In learning to apply sensation-terms to ourselves and to others we learn that the *possibility* of concealing our sensations is as central to the concept of sensation as the idea of solitary activity is to the game of patience.[15]

Without the distinction drawn at PI §243, one might see no problem in speaking intelligibly of private experience (see, e.g., Maddell 2018, 53–54). PI §248 might seem to suggest that sensations are *superprivate,* or that Wittgenstein *thinks* them so (e.g., Wellman 1962, 446). From this initial mistake others follow. Perhaps Wittgenstein allows that we *have super*private sensations but denies that we can *name* them (Strawson 1954, 86), or *express* them (Hadot 2010 [1959], 77–78) or *say* that we have them (Pitcher 1964, 298–299; Mundle 1966, 35; Gram 1971, 303) because, although *sensations* are superprivate,

---

[14] See, e.g., Malcolm 1954, 530; Geach 1957, 3; Hacker 1972, 245–246; Kenny 1973, 189–190; Hallett 1977, 319; Cavell 1979, 330–331; Gert 1986, 433; Hanfling 1989, 98; Dummett 1993a, 24; McGinn 2013 [1997], 146–147.

[15] See, e.g., Pole 1958, 68–69; Hacker 1972, 248–249; Fogelin 1987, 170; McGinn 2013 [1997], 149; Kienzler 2007, 107; Mulhall 2007, 60–61. For a similar point see Donagan 1966, 334.

language cannot be. Perhaps Wittgenstein conflates different senses of 'privacy' (Mundle 1966, 37) or holds that others might have no sensations at all (44)!

Wittgenstein's critique of private language, however, denies neither that we have sensations nor that we can speak of them to others. His target, as in late 1929, is the idea that talk of sensations is usefully modelled on talk of spatio-temporal objects.

5 Solitary Speakers

Wittgenstein's remarks about philosophy and philosophical problems (PI §§89–133) and his anti-essentialism about language-games (PI §§65–88) suggest that we should expect no lessons about the nature of language in general from his treatment of private language. Indeed, we should expect that treatment, grounded in the considerations adduced in Section 3, to criticise the objectification of sensation and perceptual appearances and its consequences for thinking about our vocabulary of sensation and perception.

Nonetheless, some commentators take Wittgenstein to hold 'that a private language contradicts general principles for the meaningful use of linguistic expressions' (Tugendhat 1986, 84) – especially the general principle that language is essentially shared. This idea was first advanced by Strawson (1954, 84), but Ayer's exchange with Rush Rhees shaped the ensuing debate.

Ayer acknowledges that a private language, for Wittgenstein, is one whose speaker 'would have no meaning to communicate even to himself' (Ayer 1954, 65), but he criticises this implied conclusion by imagining 'a Robinson Crusoe left alone while still an infant, having not yet learned to speak' (70). Young Robinson survives to invent a language to describe 'the flora and fauna of his island' (70) – empirically improbable, but not logically impossible, says Ayer. But if Crusoe can manage this, why not a language for his own sensations? Wittgenstein's argument, thinks Ayer, requires justification for one's application of a word, and that requires 'some independent test for determining that the sign is being used correctly' (Ayer 1954, 67). Such a test is supposedly unavailable in a private sensation-language, thinks Ayer, because if I cannot recognise my sensation, then there is no reason to think that I could recognise another inner episode – for example, a memory of the sensation – that could justify it. The problem, Ayer complains, is that 'unless there is something that one is allowed to recognize, no test can ever be completed: there will be no justification for the use of any sign at all' (68; cf. Ayer 1973, 95; 1986, 76). If the argument works, then *public* language is impossible. The argument thus makes a faulty presupposition – that no memory of a past sensation can justify my applying 'S' to a recurrence of this sensation. This is just scepticism about memory.

Ayer was 'on the right lines' (Hervey 1957, 71) according to some, and the impression that Wittgenstein doubted the possibility of a solitary speaker was reinforced by his early defenders, Rhees (1954, 88) and Winch (1958, 33–34).[16] Even when Crusoe goes unmentioned, his airy presence persists in the conviction that Wittgenstein has tried (perhaps, failed) to show that language is essentially shared.[17] Many later commentators endorse some version of this 'community view', motivated by something like Claudine Verheggen's complaint that if Wittgenstein is not essentially embedding meaning in communal practices, then he is not saying 'anything illuminating about the nature of language' (2007, 615).[18]

Another tradition noted the 'difference in logical character between' (Hardin 1959, 521) an isolated speaker's words and a private language as intended by Wittgenstein.[19] On this view, for Wittgenstein, an argument against private language requires only that language be in principle shareable, not necessarily shared.[20]

Wittgenstein clearly took language to be *paradigmatically* shared,[21] but finding evidence that he took language to be *necessarily* shared is more difficult.[22] Comparing linguistic practices to games is meant to discourage the thought that there is some set of necessary and sufficient conditions for applying the term 'language' (PI §65), and the metaphilosophical remarks at PI §§89–133 discourage seeking an argument with such a conclusion (Schroeder 2006, 200). As John Canfield contends, for Wittgenstein, wolf-child Crusoe would be 'a borderline case of language use' (1996, 485). If we want to describe the concept of language, we should not *start* with such improbable cases, but Wittgenstein's reluctance to circumscribe the concept sharply makes it unlikely that he means to rule them out. It is not Wittgenstein's *task* in the *Investigations*, *pace* Verheggen, to say 'anything illuminating about the nature of language' (Verheggen 2007, 615).

But what of *this* passage?

> [T]o *think* one is following a rule is not to follow a rule. And that's why it's not possible to follow a rule 'privately'; otherwise, thinking one was following a rule would be the same thing as following it. (PI §202)

---

[16] See, later, Manser 1969, 167.
[17] See Pole 1958, 75; Perkins 1965, 446–447; Gruender 1968, 203; Quine 1969, 27.
[18] E.g., Wright 1980; Peacocke 1981; Bloor 1983, 57, 1997; Kripke 1982, 110; Armstrong 1984, 61; Martin 1987, 47; Grayling 1988, 85; Sauvé 1988, 417; Malcolm 1989; Potter 1993, 163–165; Putnam 1994, 95; Koethe 1996, 139–144; Stainton 1996, 185–186; Campbell 1997, 111–112; Jacquette 1997, 216; Williams 1999, 216; Braaten 2002, 182–186; Medina 2002, 156–194, 216n220; Soames 2003, 34, 52; Martinich and Sosa 2013, 653; von Savigny 2019 [1988], 9–10.
[19] See Thomson 1964, 20; Mundle 1966, 38; Cooke 1974, 29; Bouveresse 1987 [1976], 445.
[20] See Baker and Hacker 1984; Blackburn 1984, 92; McGinn 1984, 78; Budd 1989, 40; Schulte 1992, 145; Dummett 1993b, 184; Johnston 1993, 19; Glock 1996, 309; Baker and Hacker 2014 [1985].
[21] – As is indirectly illustrated by Burns 1994.
[22] See Pears 1988, 361–388; Werhane 1989; Canfield 1996; Pears 2006, 61–63.

This remark, quoted by Kripke (1982, 3) and others, resonates with a line from the diary-example (see Sections 8, 9, and 11): 'One would like to say: whatever is going to seem correct to me is correct. And that only means that here we can't talk about "correct"' (PI §258). Supporters of the community view think that 'privately' inherits its sense here from the description of rules as '*customs*' and 'institutions' (PI §199) and 'practice[s]' (PI §202).

These terms sound plausibly communal in English, and Martin Kusch (2006, 248–252) argues that this reflects the predominant usage of the original German terms. Native anglophones may feel abashed before such claims, but some prominent germanophone interpreters are unmoved.[23] Furthermore, claims about standard use do not settle how *Wittgenstein* uses these terms. As Baker and Hacker argue, there are numerous passages in Wittgenstein's writings in which such words as 'custom' ('*Gepflogenheit*'), 'institution' ('*Institution*') and 'practice' ('*Praxis*') occur with no evident connotations of community (2014 [1985], 121–122, 140–143). The fact that 'privately' appears in scare-quotes at PI §202 emphasises that it is not *obvious* how to interpret it.[24] The remark that rule-following is a *practice* that cannot be engaged in 'privately' originally belonged to an argument for thinking that I need not *recognise* my image of red before I can judge that it is red (Ms 129, 119) – a discussion that survives as PI §§377–381 (Baker and Hacker 2014 [1985], 126–129). To interpose a moment of recognition is to treat my knowledge of my sensations and perceptual experiences as a datable achievement. But if my knowledge of my own sensations and appearances need not be such an achievement (Section 6.2) – if it could be an aspect of my linguistic competence (PI §381) – then the connection between rule-following and the critique of private language is more like this: 'there is a way of grasping a rule' for the use of a sensation-term 'which is *not* an interpretation' (PI §201) – *not*, that is, a matter of *recognising* my sensation and inferring that it should be categorised as pain or as the appearance of redness, as the objectification of sensations suggests.

Many key arguments of PI §§243–315 were developed earlier than, and independently of, the discussion of rule-following. The critiques of the misleading metaphor of phenomenal space, of the privacy and ownership of sense-data, of the objectification of sensations and appearances, of privileged access, all date from 1929 to 1936. The example of the child-genius at PI §257 first appears in *The Big Typescript* (BT, 209 v). The diary-example itself (see Sections 8, 9, and 11) originates in 'Notes for Lectures on "Private Experience" and "Sense-Data"', from 1934 to 1936, where the idea of keeping a diary of my private experiences

---

[23] See, e.g., Schulte 1992, 145; Glock 1996, 309–311; Schroeder 2006, 199–201.
[24] See Fogelin 2009, 60; Baker and Hacker 2014 [1985], 133.

appears in the context of wondering whether I could, in a private language, track recurrences of a colour-sensation, for example, of red (LPE, 234).[25] The discussion of rule-following, by contrast, largely derives from work begun around 1935 (see BBB 141–143) and mostly carried out from 1937 onward.[26] Had we independent grounds for thinking that Wittgenstein treats rules as essentially communal, we might think that the overall significance of the passages on private language had been transformed by the time of the *Investigations*, but even this would not alter their *basis* in the considerations reviewed in Section 3.

I assume, then, that the objectification of sensation and perceptual appearances, supported by the misleading metaphor of phenomenal space, and the consequences of this objectification for our thinking about sensation-language constitute the target of Wittgenstein's criticism of privacy and private language. I return briefly to Kripke (Section 10), but, otherwise, I set aside concerns about the role of community in Wittgenstein's treatment of private language.

6 Ontological Privacy, Epistemic Privacy and First-Person Authority

The distinction between 'ordinary' privacy and 'superprivacy' (Section 4) bisects the distinction (Section 3) between 'epistemic privacy' and the 'privacy of ownership' (Hacker 1972, 222). Each of the latter senses of 'private' can be interpreted in an 'ordinary' way or in a 'superprivate' way. My sensations are epistemically private in the ordinary sense when I conceal them from others, and they belong to me in the ordinary sense that 'the person who is suffering is the person who manifests pain' (PI §302) (Fogelin 1987, 170). That is what its being *my* pain amounts to. But the impulse to think of sensations as *superprivate* is expressed *epistemically* by the thought that 'only I can know whether I am really in pain; another person can only surmise it' (PI §246), and *ontologically* by the thought that 'Another person can't have my pains' (PI §253). Consider the latter first.

6.1 *My* pains

Wittgenstein's earlier concerns about the private ownership of sensations resurface at PI §253:

> 'Another person can't have my pains.' – *My* pains – what pains are they? What counts as a criterion of identity here? Consider what makes it possible in the

---

[25] Its *inspiration* seems to be *Schlick's* diary-example (1979 [1932], 307–309) – a verificationist argument against the possibility of private language, but *not* against solitary language. Nielsen (2008, 56) misreads Schlick on this point.

[26] On the sources of these passages see Baker and Hacker 2014 [1985], 33–34. On the dating of these sources see von Wright 1993, 489–492.

case of physical objects to speak of 'two exactly the same': for example, to say, 'This chair is not the one you saw here yesterday, but is exactly the same as it'.

In so far as it makes *sense* to say that my pain is the same as his, it is also possible for us both to have the same pain. (And it would also be conceivable that two people feel pain in the same – not just the corresponding – place. That might be the case with Siamese twins, for instance.)

I have seen a person in a discussion on this subject strike himself on the breast and say: 'But surely another person can't have THIS pain!' – The answer to this is that one does not define a criterion of identity by emphatically enunciating the word 'this'. Rather, the emphasis merely creates the illusion of a case in which we are conversant with such a criterion of identity, but have to be reminded of it. (PI §253)

We are not told what counts as a criterion of identity, but we are invited to compare (or contrast) criteria for the identity of physical objects with those for sensations, and one voice in the conversation tartly dismisses the suggestion that my pain can be individuated by striking my own breast. These considerations seem meant to be compatible with saying that you and I might have the same pain – at least, if it makes sense to say that my pain and yours are the same.

Few early interpreters discussed PI §253,[27] but one later critic complains that it 'betokens a pretty obvious failure to distinguish between qualitative and numerical identity' (Maddell 2018, 59). Sympathetic readers have thought that *we* are prone to such failure – that Wittgenstein meant the *qualitative* identity of sensations, not their numerical identity.[28] Both impulses liken sensations to objects.[29] When I smite my breast and say, 'THIS pain!' it is as though I tried to point to my pain as I might my heart. But unless we can both already use the word 'pain', this attempted ostension just 'emphatically enunciate[s] the word "this"'. It seems otherwise only if we think of pains as objects – albeit ones that only their actual possessor can observe or, indeed, possess.

As we have seen (Section 3), Wittgenstein resists this analogy well before the *Investigations*. If we liken the grammar of 'pain' or of 'sensation' to the grammar of colour-words, rather than the grammar of names for spatio-temporal objects,[30] then the distinction between qualitative identity and numerical identity gets no grip.

---

[27] Important exceptions are Garver 1960, 392; Cook 1965, 297, 306; Malcolm 1967, 139–146. See also Hervey 1957, 78; Pole 1958, 70.
[28] See Thornton 1969, 270; Pears 1988, 231; Lin 2017, 268; Fan 2021, 51.
[29] A related impulse distinguishes sensation-types from sensation-tokens. See Pears 1988; Jacquette 1997, 274–297; Cusmariu 2022, 203–205, 209–210.
[30] See Malcolm 1967, 140–141; Tanesini 2004, 96–97; Schroeder 2013, 202; Hymers 2017, 82–83; Kanterian 2017, 451–453. For challenges see Cavell 1969, 242–253; Hunter 1985, 126–128; Mulhall 2007, 71–83.

Wittgenstein does not categorically say that likening sensations to physical objects is *wrong* (see PI §132). (Maybe that is why he writes, 'In so far as it makes *sense* to say that my pain is the same as his . . . ' (PI §253).) We *could* adopt another grammatical convention. 'Then if I say he can't have the same toothache, that is now a proposition of grammar' (RSD, 293).[31] But it is easy to mistake this grammatical stipulation for a 'metaphysical proposition' (BBB 49) because it resembles the empirical proposition that we do not feel pain in other bodies. This empirical proposition records a 'remarkable and interesting fact' (PR §55), but it is contingent, as suggested by the case of conjoined twins (PI §253) and by the more extraordinary possibilities considered in Section 3.

Such a convention would require excluding either the ownership of sensations or the impossibility of sharing them. The argument against sense-data from 1929 thus survives into the *Investigations*. If '[a]nother person *can't* have my pains', as another person *could* have my bicycle, then *I* cannot have my pains: 'if you logically exclude other people's having something, it loses its sense to say that you have it' (PI §398). The problem lies in saying that my ownership of sensations is *like* my ownership of physical objects, while insisting that it could not be transferred to anyone else.

6.2 'I Know'

> In what sense are my sensations *private*? – Well, only I can know whether I am really in pain; another person can only surmise it. – In one way this is false, and in another nonsense. If we are using the word 'know' as it is normally used (and how else are we to use it?), then other people very often know if I'm in pain. – Yes, but all the same, not with the certainty with which I know it myself! – It can't be said of me at all (except perhaps as a joke) that I *know* I'm in pain. What is it supposed to mean – except perhaps that I *am* in pain?
>
> Other people cannot be said to learn of my sensations *only* from my behaviour – for I cannot be said to learn of them. I *have* them.
>
> This much is true: it makes sense to say about other people that they doubt whether I am in pain; but not to say it about myself. (PI §246)

The objectification of sensations and perceptual appearances encourages thinking that we know about our own sensations and perceptions in a way that is like our knowing of spatio-temporal things but also inherently superior to others' knowledge of our inner experiences. On this view I have 'privileged access' (Ryle 1949, 14) to my sensations and perceptions – I know them *directly* as you never could. My knowledge of your sensations and appearances, by contrast, is

---

[31] Pole (1958, 70) and Garver (1960, 392) think Wittgenstein *accepts* this 'proposition of grammar'.

indirect, tenuously inferred from your verbal and nonverbal behaviour (LPE 215). It then seems preposterous to suggest that I do not *know* that I am in pain.[32] However, a consideration of the grammar of ascriptions of sensation and perception weakens both these temptations. I begin with knowledge of things in space and then return to privileged access.

If sensations and appearances are objects, then we should expect our knowledge of them sometimes to be an *achievement*. I should expect sometimes to *discover* that I am in pain, perhaps after performing tests, as I discover that my body temperature is 36.7 ° C by consulting a thermometer, and I should be able to doubt the results, as I can doubt the reliability of my thermometer. The concluding sentences of PI §246 target this view, telling us that I do not *learn* of my sensations and that it makes no sense to say that I *doubt* whether I am in pain.[33] The joke about knowing I am in pain is, thus, best read as a joke about *discovering* that I am in pain.

This point is easily missed. Some commentators take Wittgenstein to argue that spontaneous, first-person uses of psychological predicates are not genuine assertions: they lack truth-values and, *therefore*, do not express knowledge.[34] But let's not be thrown off the scent. PI §247 hints that we *can* use the word 'know' to convey the certainty sought by the interlocutor at PI §246:

> 'Only you can know if you had that intention.' One might tell someone this when explaining the meaning of the word 'intention' to him. For then it means: *that* is how we use it.
> (And here 'know' means that the expression of uncertainty is senseless.)
> (PI §247)

However, knowing one's intention in this sort of case (there are others (Section 7)), like knowing that one is in pain, need *not* be seen as an epistemic achievement.[35] It does not rest on identifying one's inner state and noticing that it satisfies some criterion for being that (kind of) state. It rather resembles a default entitlement that I have as a competent speaker to express my

---

[32] E.g., Gram 1971, 309; Hacker 1972, Ch. IX; Tugendhat 1986, 115; Bouveresse 1987 [1976], 454; Snowdon 2011, 424; Maddell 2018, 59.

[33] Whether it makes sense depends on how we represent the grammar of sensation-terms. When I soak my hands, numb with cold, in hot water, is it painful or pleasurable? There may be no clear answer, but we could say that if we allow that doubt is possible, it is indeterminate what I feel.

[34] E.g., Hartnack 1965, 97–99; Emmons 1968, 416, 428; Hacker 1972, 256; Clegg 1974, 209; Robinson 1994, 93. *Perhaps* Malcolm (1954, 542–543) agrees. All presuppose a certain understanding of PI §244. See Section 7.

[35] There are other uses of 'to know,' as well, such as *acknowledging* my pain. See Cavell 1969, 255–258; Fogelin 1987, 171; Mulhall 2007, 43–53. But these do not suggest that knowing I am in pain is an achievement, after all.

sensations, perceptions or other psychological states (see PI §381).[36] The point is made explicit in the context of perceptual appearances:

> What is the criterion for the sameness of two images? – What is the criterion for the redness of an image? For me, when it's someone else's image: what he says and does. – For myself, when it's my image: nothing. And what goes for 'red' also goes for 'same'. (PI §377)

I do not judge that something looks red to me after first *recognising* my visual image: 'How do I recognize that this colour is red? –One answer would be: "I have learnt English"' (PI §381; see PI §384).

So, as Stern says (2004, 173), Wittgenstein is not endorsing a particular theory about the nature of knowledge here – just drawing attention to ways in which our talk of knowing objects does not easily transfer to our talk of knowing sensations or perceptual appearances.[37]

The example of the redness of my visual image emphasises another consequence of the objectification of sensation and perception. Where there is room for discovery there is room for identification and misidentification (see Section 12). But, although we might intelligibly say that I identify my sensation *in* its expression, it is no more plausible to suppose that my first-person uses of verbs of experience are *based on* identifying or recognising my sensations and perceptual appearances than to suppose that my *non-verbal* expressions of sensation rest on identification or recognition. Two cases illustrate this point:

> Are we perhaps over-hasty in our assumption that the smile of a baby is not pretence? – And on what experience is our assumption based?
>   (Lying is a language-game that needs to be learned like any other one.)
>   Why can't a dog simulate pain? Is it too honest? Could one teach a dog to simulate pain? Perhaps it is possible to teach it to howl on particular occasions as if it were in pain, even when it isn't. But the right surroundings for this behaviour to be real simulation would still be missing. (PI §§249–250)

---

[36] Being a competent speaker is another kind of achievement.

[37] I do not imply that knowing spatio-temporal objects always involves moments of recognition that are absent from knowing sensations, but we *sometimes mis*recognise objects, and they have properties about which we may be ignorant or mistaken. So knowledge of objects *can* be an achievement. Wittgenstein later argues that in some contexts I can no more doubt that I have two hands than that I am in pain (when I am). Like the case of pain, some of these cases involve the speaker's linguistic competence: 'If I wanted to doubt whether this was my hand, how could I avoid doubting whether the word "hand" has any meaning?' (OC §369). But, although in some important contexts such doubts are pragmatically, even semantically, self-defeating (see Hymers 2010, 174–190), in others they are not. Awakening after a serious accident, I may intelligibly doubt whether I have two hands. More prosaically, I can doubt that I have enough cash to pay my cab-fare, and I can alleviate or confirm that doubt by opening my wallet. But how would I check – or doubt – whether it is pain that I feel after a cinder block falls on my foot?

A smile naturally expresses joy or pleasure. To imagine an infant *feigning* pleasure is to imagine the infant's having learned the concept of pleasure and its natural expression and to mimic that natural expression when there is no pleasure. Such pretence comes later. And the dog apparently feigning pain *need* not have learned the concept of pain but simply to produce behaviour that mimics pain's natural expression, in response to training.

PI §246 also suggests that, although others *can* sometimes doubt whether I am in pain, this is not because they are at a disadvantage in learning about my sensations (because *I* do not learn about them at all). I can sometimes conceal my pain, but your mistaken belief about my sensation can be corrected if I reveal the truth or if you talk to my family or surreptitiously observe my behaviour. (My pain is sometimes private but not *superprivate*.) On other occasions hiding our pain from each other hardly seems possible. When you hammer your thumb, your pain is as accessible to me as a dazzling sunrise or a clap of thunder. 'Just try – in a real case – to doubt someone else's fear or pain!' (PI §303). So 'other people very often know if I am in pain'.

6.3 An Undoubted Asymmetry

The idea that I know my own sensations and perceptual appearances directly and yours only indirectly – that I can only 'surmise' that you are in pain – is attractive also because it seems to *explain* what Donald Davidson (1984) calls 'first-person authority'. When it comes to psychological vocabulary, 'My attitude to my own words is wholly different from that of others' (PPF §103). If I complain that I have knee-pain, it would be absurd for my doctor to ask, 'Are you sure?' but you might reasonably raise doubts if I say that my *neighbour* has knee-pain. (Something else might explain her gait.) I have authority in ascribing psychological predicates to myself. If I say that I have a headache or that this shade of red looks darker to me than that one, I expect others to defer to me.[38] By contrast, if I ascribe those predicates to you, I expect no automatic deferral from my interlocutor, and your denial will erase my slate of claims.

The doctrine of privileged access treats this ordinary deference of others to my psychological self-ascriptions as justified by my access to evidence that others lack. Others can have only 'indirect' evidence of my sensations, perceptions, thoughts and so on by observing my behaviour and listening to my words (LPE, 215; NPL, 448). So even if I *can* doubt what sensations I have, I remain better placed than others to know them.

---

[38] This authority, particularly with respect to emotions and intentional attitudes, can be undermined by imbalances in social power. See Campbell 1997, 135–164.

The most extreme version of this idea is the solipsist's temptation 'to say that only my own experience is real: "I know that *I* see, hear, feel pains, etc., but not that anyone else does. I can't know this because I am I and they are they"' (BBB, 46). But if, as Wittgenstein's critique of the private ownership of sensations suggests, there is no meaningful way to isolate *my experiences* if someone else cannot have them, then my alleged capacity to report with privilege on the contents of *my* private experience cannot explain first-person authority.[39]

To understand first-person authority in terms of privileged access is to understand it as *robustly* epistemic – as a recurrent achievement. But if my ordinary knowledge that I am in pain is not like this, then neither is first-person authority. It is more like an entitlement that reflects my capacity to use first-person psychological predicates. This idea attracts Wittgenstein as early as 1929 when he imagines translating psychological vocabulary into a language without first-person pronouns.

> [I]f I, L. W., have toothache, then that is expressed by means of the proposition 'There is toothache'. But if that is so, what we now express by the proposition 'A has toothache' is put as follows: 'A is behaving as L. W. does when there is toothache'. (PR §58)

Such a language 'could have anyone at all at its centre', and so there is nothing in its vocabulary that captures the 'privileged status' of 'the language with me at its centre' (PR §58). Its special status for me must lie in its *application* (PR §58), not in its supposed capacity to describe what I know immediately. What is special about first-person pronouns in the context of 'verbs of experience' (RPP I §836), then, must lie in their first-person applications – not in some special power they have infallibly to describe 'immediate experience' (PR §57).

In the *Blue Book*, Wittgenstein experiments with clarifying such applications by distinguishing the 'use as subject' from the 'use as object' (BBB, 66) of first-person pronouns,[40] but his interest shifts in his 'Notes for Lectures on "Private Experience" and "Sense-Data"', where he writes, 'There seems to be an undoubted asymmetry in the use of the word "to see" (and all words relating to personal experience)' (LPE, 215).[41] To insist that 'my reason for saying that I see is not the observation of my behaviour' (LPE, 215) is not to insist that I have *direct* epistemic access to my sensations and perceptions; it is, rather, to formulate 'a gramm[atical] prop[osition]' (LPE, 215). This remains his mature view:

---

[39] '[S]olipsism strictly carried out coincides with pure realism' (TLP 5.64). See Pears 1988, 226–269; Stern 1995, 72–87.
[40] See Hymers 2017, 87–88, 101–102.
[41] Bloor (1983, 51) thinks Wittgenstein *denies* the asymmetry.

Psychological verbs characterized by the fact that the third person of the present is to be identified by observation, the first person not.

Sentences in the third person of the present: information. In the first person present, expression. ((Not quite right.)) (RPP II §63)

Think of paradigmatic utterances of 'I am in pain' not as *descriptions* based on observations but as spontaneous *expressions* – avowals – that resemble moans and grimaces. This is the linguistic correlate of the thought that my knowledge of my own sensations is not ordinarily an achievement, and it presents an alternative to thinking of my first-person authority as rooted in privileged access to my inner states. It also helps undermine our temptation to objectify (see Section 3) sensations and perceptual appearances.

7 Avowals

If sensations are objects, then they should get their names as objects do, albeit in private, phenomenal space. PI §244 tries to distract our gaze from this picture:

> How do words *refer* to sensations? – There doesn't seem to be any problem here; don't we talk about sensations every day, and name them? But how is the connection between the name and the thing named set up? This question is the same as: How does a human being learn the meaning of names of sensations? For example, of the word 'pain'. Here is one possibility: words are connected with the primitive, natural, expressions of sensation and used in their place. A child has hurt himself and he cries; then adults talk to him and teach him exclamations and, later, sentences. They teach the child new pain-behaviour.
>
> 'So you are saying that the word "pain" really means crying?' – On the contrary: the verbal expression of pain replaces crying, it does not describe it. (PI §244)

Such first-person, expressive uses of psychological vocabulary are known as 'avowals'.[42] An avowal of my pain is a spontaneous, articulate expression of it – for example, 'That hurts!' or 'I am in pain!' Wittgenstein describes such uses of psychological vocabulary as 'wrung from us – like a cry' (PI §546). They are not assertions or descriptions in the sense of being based on evidence or observation of my sensations. 'It is not, of course, that I identify my sensation by means of criteria; it is, rather, that I use the same expression' (PI §290).

If we assume that only *assertions* – or expressions of *belief* – are truth-apt, then it may seem that avowals can be neither true nor false. However, we need not make this assumption.[43] The antecedents of conditional statements are

---

[42] Ryle 1949, 98 inspires this term.
[43] See Jacobsen 1997. Nor is it clear that Wittgenstein accepted it. See Kenny 1973, 196–201; Tugendhat 1986, 109; Glock 1996, 53; Jacobsen 1996, 21–31.

truth-apt, but, being conditional, they assert nothing and express no belief. To say of the antecedent of a conditional that it can be true or false is to say, roughly, that another token-sentence of the same type can be used to make an assertion. So if 'I am in pain' can be uttered as an assertion, then its occurrence as an avowal is compatible with its being truth-apt.[44]

But does PI §244 leave room for first-person, present-tense, indicative uses of verbs of experience that are *not* avowals? Some have thought not,[45] but Wittgenstein does not 'deny that first-person sentences about sensations may ... be more or less like natural expressions of sensation' (Malcolm 1954, 542). They are *less* like natural expressions of sensation when they are *more* like descriptions of sensation.[46] When I learn to supplement spontaneous natural expressions of pain with verbal expressions like 'I am in pain', 'it is not as if the language-game *ends* with this: it begins with it' (PI §290). In his 1936 lectures Wittgenstein says that '"toothache" is not *only* a substitute for moaning. But it is *also* a substitute for moaning ... ' (RSD, 298). He later extends the point to fear:[47]

> A cry is not a description. But there are intermediate cases. And the words 'I am afraid' may approximate more, or less, to being a cry. They may come very close to one, and also be *very* far removed from it.
>
> We surely do not invariably say that someone is *complaining* because he says he is in pain. So the words 'I am in pain' may be a cry of complaint, and may be something else. (PPF ix §§83–84)[48]

A complaint in this case is an avowal, an expression of my pain, but not every utterance of 'I am in pain' is an avowal. This, I suggest, is the point of Wittgenstein's remark that his description of first-person, present-tense psychological ascriptions as expressive is 'Not quite right' (RPP II §63).

Other readers have suggested that Wittgenstein is committed to an expressivist *theory* of sensation-talk.[49] Such a theory *might* look roughly like this: pain and some other sensations (nausea, itching, etc.) have characteristic natural expressions.[50] Learning terms for these sensations, I learn to replace or

---

[44] The situation is less complex than with 'expressivist' views about ethical propositions, according to which apparent assertions about what is right or wrong are really expressions of the speaker's *attitude* and are, therefore, not truth-apt.

[45] See Strawson 1954, 86–88; Stern 1963, 748n3; Olscamp 1965, 240; Mundle 1966, 35; Manser 1969, 176; Clegg 1974, 212–213; Maddell 2018, 58–59.

[46] See, e.g., Geach 1957, 121–122; Passmore 1957, 433; Holborow 1967, 352–353; Cornman 1968, 118; Kenny 1973, 199; Sauvé 1985, 10; Hacker 2019a [1990], 121–125; Johnston 1993, 25; Glock 1996, 52; Connelly 2013, 567–568; Tang 2014, 3185–3191; Hymers 2017, 92–93.

[47] See Szabados 1981.   [48] See also LW I §899; LW II 22; RPP I §479; RPP II §§728, 735.

[49] See, e.g., Geach 1957, 121–122; Cook 1972, 43–44; Fogelin 1987, 169–170; Jacobsen 1996, 14–17; Fogelin 2009, 64n2; Tang 2014, 3186, 2015, 112.

[50] Not all sensations have natural behavioural expressions, nor did Wittgenstein think so (contra Maddell 2018, 59; Lin 2021, 152), as many commentators have noted: Rembert 1975, 237–238;

supplement their natural expressions with articulate first-person, present-tense verbal expressions that make use of these terms. My expressive uses of these sensation-terms involve no intermediate step of identifying or recognising my sensations, any more than my spontaneous non-verbal behaviour does. (We could say that my sensation is identified in the act of my expressing it.[51]) However, I learn to treat these natural expressions in others as grounds for ascribing the same sensations to them, and their avowals of pain also serve me as grounds for such ascriptions. What I ascribe to myself without grounds I ascribe to others on behavioural grounds, verbal or non-verbal. Because my verbal expressions of sensation are made with declarative sentences, they are truth-apt, and they can play a role in inferences. From my expressive utterances of 'I am in pain!' you can infer 'He is in pain.'[52] Having learned how to express (and describe) my pain, I can then apply these lessons to other sensations that lack natural expressions.[53]

We find hints of such a view in the early 1930s (DS, 51).[54] Wittgenstein's lecture notes from 1934 to 1936 are more explicit (LPE 254, 261, 262, 281).[55] Further support appears at PI §§256 and 288, and other remarks from the 1940s reinforce the impression:

> Primitive pain-behaviour is a sensation-behaviour; it gets replaced by a linguistic expression. 'The word "pain" is the name of a sensation' is equivalent to '"I've got a pain" is an expression of sensation'. (RPP I §313)

Against attributing an expressivist theory to Wittgenstein are his warnings against 'advanc[ing] any kind of theory' (PI §109) in philosophy, where our task is to clarify the grammar of expressions that lead us into confusion (PI §§122–133). When he introduces the idea that a child learns to replace natural expressions of sensation with a verbal expression, he simply calls it 'one possibility' (PI §244).[56]

Malcolm 1977, 101; Kripke 1982, 104n; Gert 1986, 410–411; Hacker 2019a [1990], 121; Mulhall 2007, 25–26; Tang 2015, 108n8. See also RPP II §63. 'The vast majority of our desires have no natural, pre-linguistic behavioural expression', though 'their expression is nevertheless rooted in the primitive behaviour of striving to get or crying for something or other' (Hacker 2019a [1990], 121).

[51] See Price 1973, 49–67.   [52] For an alternative see Hacker 2019a [1990], 268.
[53] For more see Hacker 2019a [1990], 117–125; Hymers 2017, 97–120. Cf. Bar-On 2004.
[54] His example here is fear. Compare: 'One doesn't shout "Help" because he observes his own state of fear' (RPP II §724).
[55] See also NPL, 449.
[56] See Malcolm 1954, 538–540; Levin 1973, 205–206; Cooke 1974, 34; Rembert 1975, 238; Finch 1977, 133; Hallett 1977, 322; Bloor 1983, 51; Dunlop 1984, 354; Pears 1988, 358; Stern 1995, 181, 2004, 172–173; Baker 2004, 113, 121, 123, 126, 133; Mulhall 2007, 38–40; Hymers 2010, 151, 2017, 119–120; McGinn 2013 [1997], 143.

However, the temptation to elaborate on this suggestion, as earlier, is compatible with thinking that Wittgenstein was not advancing a general theory. Part of the task of dispelling philosophical confusion is to clarify the grammar of the expressions that puzzle us. Wittgenstein's remarks on first-person, present-tense psychological ascriptions aim at such clarity (see Hacker 2019a [1990], 117–121). Moreover, to claim that the suggestion of PI §244 is a *possibility* is still to assume a certain burden of argument. One might try to discharge that burden by saying that the proposal is *at least* as plausible as the view that the meanings of sensation-terms are fixed by inner ostensive definition[57] (see Sections 9 and 11). Or one might try to support the claim of possibility by exploring the proposal in greater detail. What matters for Wittgenstein's purposes is that the view be sufficiently plausible to suggest that the inner-ostension account is not obligatory.

8 The First Wave: Verification and Memory

The first commentator to mention 'the private-language argument' in print was Héctor-Neri Castañeda (1962),[58] but I assume it was already common to speak of Wittgenstein's discussion this way. To do so is typically to assume that there is a central argument – usually sought in the diary-example of PI §258, aided by some other passages – and that this argument aims to demonstrate the logical impossibility of a private language.[59] I reject both these assumptions, but it is important to understand their pervasive influence on the reception of Wittgenstein's work.

Castañeda attributes the argument also to Norman Malcolm, whom he regards as a reliable expositor of Wittgenstein's views. Malcolm is certainly among the most sensitive and astute of First-Wave readers of the *Investigations*, and his influential interpretation fuels the idea that Wittgenstein's critique is a sustained argument against the logical possibility of such a language – a *reductio ad absurdum* (1954, 537) of the idea that there might be a language that 'cannot be understood by anyone other than the speaker' (530–531). The significance of this reasoning, thinks Malcolm, is far-reaching, challenging 'the philosophy of Descartes and ... the theory of ideas of classical British empiricism as well as ... recent and contemporary phenomenalism and sense-datum theory' (1954, 531).

---

[57] Baker 2004, 134; Stern 2004, 172. [58] Nielsen (2008, 80n20) confirms my claim.
[59] See, e.g., Malcolm 1954, 537; Heath 1956, 70; Passmore 1957, 432–433; Castañeda 1962, 96; Gram 1971, 298; Berger 1971, 87; Blackburn 1984, 92–93; Pears 1988, 329; Tugendhat 1989, 88; Jacquette 1997, 275; Maslin 2001, 220, 228–229; Law 2004, 159, 168; Rundle 2009, 134; Churchland 2013, 91–93.

Malcolm's focus on the diary-example of PI §258 (supplemented by PI §§259, 265) has dominated the literature:

> Let's imagine the following case. I want to keep a diary about the recurrence of a certain sensation. To this end I associate it with the sign 'S' and write this sign in a calendar for every day on which I have the sensation. – I first want to observe that a definition of the sign cannot be formulated. – But all the same, I can give one to myself as a kind of ostensive definition! – How? Can I point to the sensation? – Not in the ordinary sense. But I speak, or write the sign down, and at the same time I concentrate my attention on the sensation – and so, as it were, point to it inwardly. – But what is this ceremony for? For that is all it seems to be! A definition serves to lay down the meaning of a sign, doesn't it? – Well, that is done precisely by concentrating my attention; for in this way I commit to memory the connection between the sign and the sensation. – But 'I commit it to memory' can only mean: this process brings it about that I remember the connection *correctly* in the future. But in the present case, I have no criterion of correctness. One would like to say: whatever is going to seem correct to me is correct. And that only means that here we can't talk about 'correct'. (PI §258)

I take the diary-example to make the *semantic* point that *no rule for the use of 'S' has been established* (see Section 11). However, Malcolm helps plant the seeds of two popular misunderstandings of this passage: that it aims to show the impossibility of (1) *verifying* (2) the private speaker's *memory* of how to apply a term in a private language (1954, 532). On Malcolm's *epistemic* reading, I try to define the word 'pain' privately. However, my private definition succeeds only if it ensures that my future uses of 'pain' are *consistent* with my attempted definition (532). Wittgenstein's objection, thinks Malcolm, is that I cannot 'prove' or 'confirm' (532) such consistency in the circumstances imagined. There would be no discernible 'difference between my having used [the word] consistently and its *seeming* to me that I have' (532), so the concept of correctness would not apply. I would have only '*impressions* of rules' (PI §259) governing my use of the word.

Why can nothing prove the consistency of my later use of 'pain' with my definition? I can rely only on my memory, and here my memory cannot be tested for correctness by comparing it to something independent (Malcolm 1954, 533–534).[60] Malcolm calls on PI §265 for support:

> –'But surely I can appeal from one memory to another. For example, I don't know if I have remembered the time of departure of a train right and to check it I call to mind how a page of the time-table looked. Isn't it the same here?' – No; for this process has got to produce a memory which is actually *correct*. If

---
[60] Cf. Strawson 1954, 84–85.

> the mental image of the time-table could not itself be *tested* for correctness, how could it confirm the correctness of the first memory? (As if someone were to buy several copies of the morning paper to assure himself that what it said was true.) (PI §265; Anscombe's translation[61])

I cannot confirm the correctness of my memory-impression, because the sensation is long-gone, and I cannot appeal to anyone else's memory to confirm mine. Without this possibility of confirmation, says Malcolm, 'there would not be, in the private language, any *conception* of what would establish a memory as correct' (1954, 534). Talk of correctness would be meaningless.

Malcolm did not intend to saddle Wittgenstein with a verifiability theory of meaning, but, as Thomson (1964, 29–31) complained, it is difficult to distinguish talk of 'checking one memory against another' (Malcolm 1954, 533) from saying that my memories must be verifiable for there to be any fact about how I should employ my sensation-terms. As we saw (Section 5), that demand, which Ayer thinks is the conclusion of the argument, reduces to a scepticism about memory that would apply equally to public language.

These epistemic themes – verificationism and memory-scepticism – set the agenda for commentators for two decades. Many critics followed Ayer, arguing that Wittgenstein's objections to private language 'arise from the rejection of memory rather than from the privacy of experience' (Wellman 1959, 225),[62] or complaining that 'Wittgenstein dogmatically presupposes the verifiability theory of meaning even though one of his main theses is its inadequacy' (230). Others, following Malcolm's exposition, criticised Wittgenstein for confusing a speaker's 'inability to verify his recollection of the meaning of [sensation-term] "*E*" with inability to understand what it would be for his recollection to be right' (Donagan 1966, 339),[63] and some reproduced Ayer's conclusion that 'Wittgenstein's private language argument [is] open to a *reductio*' (Stocker 1966, 47) because memories of public events are no more 'checkable' (50) than memories of private ones.[64]

Sympathetic commentators inadvertently *bolstered* the verificationist interpretation. According to Ambrose, in a private sensation-language 'there is no check on one's apparent memory that *this* is the same as what one had before' (1954, 115).[65] Geach, denying that Wittgenstein is a verificationist, contends

---

[61] Hintikka (1969, 424–425) notes a mistake in Anscombe's translation (later corrected by Hacker and Schulte) that influences Malcolm and other First-Wave interpreters. What 'the process has got to produce' is not 'a memory which is actually *correct*' but 'the *correct* memory'.

[62] See Hervey 1957, 71; Pole 1958; Hardin 1959, 521; Mundle 1966; Kultgen 1968, 40–41; Gram 1971, 313–316. Stern 1963 mentions neither Ayer nor Malcolm.

[63] See Todd 1962; Cornman 1968.

[64] See Emmons 1968; Klein 1969, 325–326. J. N. Findlay (1955, 178) anticipates both the converse of this point and a criticism of the 'community view'.

[65] She adds, 'in fact there are no criteria for "the same"' (Ambrose 1954, 115), but is this premise or conclusion?

that he rejected the possibility of giving sensation-terms 'a private *sense* ... by just attending to one's own pain-experiences, a performance that would be private and *uncheckable*' (1957, 3–4; my emphasis).[66] Other sensitive readers emphasise the importance of 'criteria for *distinguishing* the correct from the incorrect use of language' (Linsky 1957, 287; my emphasis), without which 'the undertaking [to use a sensation-term in the same way] would be empty because you could never *know* whether you had fulfilled it or not' (Garver 1960, 394; my emphasis).[67]

9 The Second Wave: Ostensive Definition

Hints of the verificationist interpretation remain long after the First Wave subsides,[68] and with them two philosophical problems: (1) the verifiability theory of meaning seems mistaken; (2) the considerations about memory overflow the banks of private language and flood the vast plains of public language.

The *interpretative* problem is that the diary-example makes a *semantic* argument, not an *epistemic* one. A clear articulation of this point was needed to exonerate Wittgenstein of the philosophical errors. Some criticisms of the verificationist interpretation appeared in the 1970s,[69] but the philosophical world had moved on to other controversies, and philosophers at large took little notice of the 'Second Wave' of interpreters. Generations of philosophers[70] remain familiar only with verificationist, often behaviourist, interpretations of Wittgenstein and with variations on Kripke's reading of the *Investigations* (the crest of the Third Wave).

The charge of memory-scepticism, however, generated important early responses, which *suggest* a semantic alternative to the verificationist reading. Rhees replied to Ayer that the discussion of private language concerned 'not a question of whether I can trust my memory,' but 'a question of when it makes sense to speak of remembering; either of a good memory or a faulty one' (1954, 83). Wittgenstein was not arguing that, without a reliable memory, there would be no criterion for correctly using a private sensation-term but

---

[66] See also Carney 1960, 561–562.
[67] See Hartnack 1965, 91–100; Saunders and Henze 1967, 37, 46ff.; Pears 1971, 159.
[68] See, e.g., Levin 1973, 204–205; Sauvé 1985, 6–7; Ayer 1986, 75–80; Temkin 1986, 109; Fogelin 1987, 179–183; Sauvé 1988, 426–427; Schulte 1992, 145; Johnston 1993, 19; Cook 1994, 319; Robinson 1994, 95–104; Wilson 1998, 30–42; Maslin 2001, 228–229; Soames 2003, 44–45; Papineau 2011, 181–182; Sluga 2011, 73; Klagge 2016, 80; Lin 2017, 269–274; Madell 2018, 54–55. Pears (1971, 159; 1988, 342–345) claims verifiability is needed for *learning*, not for *meaning*. (Cf. Fogelin 1987, 175–179 and Glock 1996, 312.) This seems *empirically* plausible, but it does not make private language *impossible*.
[69] E.g., Villanueva (1972); Clegg (1974).
[70] See, e.g., Tanner 1986; Robinson 1994, 91–118; Churchland 2013, 91–93.

that, without a criterion for correct use, there would be *no such thing as remembering*.⁷¹ This insight was best formulated by Les Holborow, who explained that to say that the private speaker has 'no criterion of correctness', is 'not to cast doubt on the accuracy or reliability of the diarist's memory. Wittgenstein is claiming not that he might misremember the criterion that he has, just for this instant, fixed; but that he has not by this ceremony fixed any criterion at all' (1967, 347).

The point is pursued by Peter Hacker (1972) and by Anthony Kenny (1973).⁷² Like First-Wave interpreters, both think there is a *central argument* aimed at demonstrating that a private language is *impossible* (Hacker 1972, 215; Kenny 1973, 178), and, like Malcolm, both think that this aim matters because 'several traditional and influential theories' (Kenny 1973, 179) in epistemology and the philosophy of mind entail the possibility of such a language (see Kenny 1966; Hacker 1972, 216–217).

However, Kenny and Hacker see clearly that a private language is one whose 'words have acquired their meaning for each of us by an essentially private process: an internal ostensive definition . . . ' (Kenny 1973, 179). Its privacy is thus unrelated to the possibility of a solitary speaker (Hacker 1972, 222). Moreover, Kenny insists that the key passages do not present a verificationist argument (1973, 195) and do not concern the reliability of memory (191–192; see Hacker 1972, 236–237).

Belief in the possibility of a private language, says Kenny, rests on the mistaken beliefs that experience is (super)private and that meaning can be given solely by ostensive definition (1973, 180; cf. Hacker 1972, 215–216). The second mistake is criticised by Wittgenstein's discussion of naming, ostensive definition, and ostensive teaching (PI §§27–36), and the upshot, says Kenny, is that 'bare ostension without training in the use of words could [not] constitute the teaching of a language' (1973, 180; see Hacker 1972, 235).

If this result is established early in the *Investigations*, it may seem that the impossibility of a private language is included as a special case. However, Kenny suggests, an aspiring private speaker might argue that, even if such considerations undermined the possibility of a language whose 'words were *learnt from* private sensations by bare ostension' (1973, 180), they would not thereby rule out the possibility of a language whose 'words *referred to* private sensations' (180), because such a language might be learned 'by some private analogue of training in the use of words' (180–181).⁷³

---

⁷¹ See Carney 1960, 562. Malcolm (1954, 534), says something similar, but his justification *looks* verificationist.
⁷² See also Goldberg 1971, 89; Senchuk 1976, 233.   ⁷³ See Tugendhat 1986, 89.

I find no such analogue mentioned in Wittgenstein's text.[74] However, Kenny thinks that his reading ensures that the discussion of private ostension is not superfluous (1973, 181). Like Malcolm, Kenny regards PI §258 as the 'kernel' (190) of the argument, but he thinks that Malcolm and others misunderstand the role of memory:

> Wittgenstein is not arguing 'When next I call something "S" how will I know it really is S?' He is arguing 'When next I call something "S" how will I know what I mean by "S"'? Even to think *falsely* that something is S I must know the meaning of 'S'; and this is what Wittgenstein argues is impossible in the private language. (192)

Saying that 'I have no criterion of correctness' (PI §258) may suggest that some *test* of the *reliability* of my memory is unavailable to me. But, really, as Holborow (1967, 147) argued, to lack a criterion of correctness is for there to be *nothing to remember* because there is no fact about what I mean by 'S' (cf. Hacker 1972, 234–235).[75]

Kenny appeals to the railway-timetable example of PI §265, but, again, his reading differs from Malcolm's. In the timetable example I check my memory of my train's departure-time by recalling a memory-image of a page from the timetable, and the question is why the private speaker could not do something comparable – recall a memory of a correlation between 'S' and S to confirm that 'S' is correctly applied. The table that we are to imagine matches terms in a would-be private language with memories of sensations.

> Let us imagine a table, something like a dictionary, that exists only in our imagination. A dictionary can be used to justify the translation of a word X by a word Y. But are we also to call it a justification if such a table is to be looked up only in the imagination? – 'Well, yes; then it is a subjective justification.' – But justification consists in appealing to an independent authority. (PI §265)

The private speaker responds that, if I wonder whether I have remembered the application of 'S' correctly, then I can check by calling the table to mind. That will confirm whether I am using 'S' as I did earlier. But when I try to test my memory of the sensation by comparing it with my memory-image of the translation-table, I must know with *which line* in the table to compare my memory. '[T]his procedure must … actually call forth the *correct* memory' (PI §265).[76] In the case of the railway timetable, which line in the table I *should*

---

[74] Nor does Wrisley 2011, 492, but Blackburn (1984, 92–103) might be taken to offer one. Perhaps Kenny means merely to imagine a possibility.

[75] Lin (2017, 261) misinterprets Kenny and Hacker on this point.

[76] Kenny avoids the translation-error that misled Malcolm (Section 8) into thinking I must recall a memory that is 'actually correct'.

take to confirm or disconfirm my memory is determined by the scheduled departure-time of my train. If I travel from Halifax to Quebec City on a Wednesday, I call a memory-image of the table to mind, see where Halifax is listed and see what departure-time is given. This is the right memory-image to consult if it accurately reproduces the published timetable.[77] But which line of my translation-table of sensation-terms should I use? My finding that line presupposes that I know which sensation to pair with which term, but if I knew that, I would not *need* the table. '[T]here can be no real looking up to see which sample goes with "S". All there can be is *remembering* which sample goes with "S", i.e. remembering what "S" means. But this is precisely what the table was supposed to confirm' (Kenny 1973, 192–193; cf. Hacker 1972, 236).

Kenny and Hacker correctly shift the problem of private language from the epistemic dimension (could a private diarist correctly remember recurring sensations?) into the semantic (has the private diarist given a sensation a name and established rules for its use?). However, their continued emphasis of PI §§258 and 265 muffles the importance of Wittgenstein's discussion of ostensive definition. Nearly a decade would pass before the importance of this shift was appreciated, and the influence of that appreciation was diluted by the storm surge of the Third Wave.

10 The Third Wave: Rules

Saul Kripke's *Wittgenstein on Rules and Private Language* (1982) captured the imaginations of philosophers who had lost interest in the debates of the First Wave, if they had ever followed them, and who had ignored the Second Wave. I have already criticised the 'community view' (Section 5) of which Kripke's view is a species, and his view focuses on rule-following, not sensation-language, but it requires further consideration because Kripke maintains that 'the real "private language argument"' (1982, 3) occurs not at PI §§243–315 but in the discussion of rules.

Kripke interprets Wittgenstein as a sceptic about the possibility of following a rule, surveying one proposal after another concerning what '*fact* about me' (1982, 21) would determine that I was following, for example, the rule for addition, rather than some eccentric rule whose observance would supply the same results over a range of cases (e.g., involving small numbers) but produce radically different results if applied in cases that, contingently, I never consider (e.g., sums involving extremely large numbers). Facts about me that might seem to settle the question, but ultimately fail, include my actual behaviour, my

---

[77] A mistake in the published timetable would complicate the example but not fundamentally alter it.

behavioural dispositions, my having the feeling of understanding when trying to apply the rule, my associating some mental image with the rule, my intending to continue the series in the same way as its earlier terms have been presented to me, and my having an interpretation of the rule. When no fact about me can be found to determine which rule I follow, Kripke's Wittgenstein concludes that there *is no such fact*. Insofar as meaning something by my words requires me to follow rules, 'It seems that the entire idea of meaning vanishes into thin air' (22). This meaning-scepticism is entirely general, so 'The "private language argument" as applied to *sensations* is only a special case of much more general considerations about language previously argued ... ' (3).

How can we accept this sceptical result about meaning? Kripke's Wittgenstein adopts a sceptical solution: although it is neither true nor false that I follow any rule, it may be *assertible* that I follow a rule, provided my teachers and peers are satisfied with my results and provided assertions about that rule have a role to play in our practices (Kripke 1982, 77–78). That description of assertibility-conditions rules out private language: without a community of ostensible rule-followers, I cannot be asserted to follow a rule because it is assertible of me that I do, only if my results are taken to agree with those of *others*. 'The impossibility of a private language emerges as a corollary of [Wittgenstein's] sceptical solution to his own paradox ... ' (68). The remarks ordinarily taken to provide the critique of private language, says Kripke, 'deal with the *application* of the general conclusions about language drawn in §§138–242 to the problem of sensations' (79). That explains, he says, why Wittgenstein–in the thick of his discussion of rules–remarks that 'it's not possible to follow a rule "privately"' (PI §202).

Not just private sensation-terms are ruled out, but any private rule-following. This, in one sense, includes Ayer's Crusoe and, in another, does not: 'The falsity of the private model need not mean that a *physically isolated* individual cannot be said to follow rules; rather that an individual, *considered in isolation* (whether or not he is physically isolated), cannot be said to do so' (Kripke 1982, 110).

Kripke neither espouses the scepticism or its sceptical solution, nor univocally attributes them to Wittgenstein (Kripke 1982, 5), but many have since done the latter. I cannot make a proper case against reading Wittgenstein this way here, so I limit myself to a few observations.[78] First, Wittgenstein's discussion of rule-following is better read as casting doubt on reductive accounts of rule-following or meaning. On this reading, it is *theories* of meaning that lead to Kripke's sceptical results, and since we evidently *do* follow rules

---

[78] See Hymers 2010, 129–149 for more, much of it inspired by Baker and Hacker 1984.

and make meaningful utterances, meaning and rule-following are no more suitable objects of deep explanatory theories than are cups and saucers. 'The meaning of a word is what an explanation of its meaning explains' (PI §560) – a clarification in context, not a general theory.

Kripke thinks that the discussion of rule-following culminates in scepticism about the possibility of meaning and rule-following:

> This was our paradox: no course of action could be determined by a rule, because every course of action can be brought into accord with the rule. The answer was: if every course of action can be brought into accord with the rule, then it can also be brought into conflict with it. And so there would be neither accord nor conflict here. (PI §201)

But, notoriously, he ignores the next paragraph:

> That there is a misunderstanding here is shown by the mere fact that in this chain of reasoning we place one interpretation behind another, as if each one contented us at least for a moment, until we thought of yet another lying behind it. For what we thereby show is that there is a way of grasping a rule which is *not* an interpretation, but which, from case to case of application, is exhibited in what we call 'following the rule' and 'going against it'. (PI §201)

Only then do we learn that '"following a rule" is a practice' (PI §202) and, therefore, not private. The sceptical conclusion is taken to rest on a misunderstanding, and, although something must be said about this anticipation of the theme of privacy (see Section 5), this does not entail that the real private language argument has already been made.

Kripke formulated his view as early as 1962–63,[79] but some of his key points are made by other commentators.[80] Most importantly, Robert Fogelin presents Wittgenstein as offering a 'sceptical solution' to 'sceptical doubts' (1976, 143; 1987, 161) about the possibility of following a rule, and this sceptical solution undergirds what Fogelin later calls the 'training argument', which he thinks 'establishes the contingent impossibility of a private language' (1987, 175). Like Kripke, Fogelin began formulating his views in the early 1960s (1987, 241n10), and, also like Kripke, Fogelin suggests that '... Wittgenstein's reasons for saying that obeying a rule is a practice provide the framework for examining the possibility of a private language' (1976, 154; 1987, 167).[81] However, Fogelin finds *several* arguments against private language.

---

[79] Von Morstein (1980) responds to Kripke's 1977 presentation in Banff, Alberta.
[80] See, e.g., Pole 1958, 75; Perkins 1965, 455–459; Hodges 1976. Kimball (1980, 411) argues against private language from the premise that one cannot obey rules privately but cites *no* passages about rule-following.
[81] Fogelin (2009) offers a very different interpretation.

First, Fogelin sees Wittgenstein's discussion of privacy and certainty at PI §§244–248 as attempting 'to diagnose the influences that make it seem natural to hold' (1976, 159; 1987, 172) that our everyday sensation-talk might be logically private. This, however, involves no attempt to demonstrate the logical impossibility of a private language.

The second and third lines of argument appear in the diary-example and the case of the human manometer at PI §270 (see Section 12). One of these, the 'public-check argument' (1987, 175), is a variation on Malcolm's reading of PI §§258 and 265, which, we have seen (Section 8), does not rule out a private language any more than a public language. However, like Kenny and Hacker, Fogelin also notes Wittgenstein's discussion of ostensive definition at PI §§27–36. The diary-example, he thinks, shows that the supposition that I might name a private sensation, merely by focusing my attention on it, illicitly presupposes a complex background of public language, without which it would be mysterious how the term 'S' could designate anything.

This additional reasoning does not refute the logical possibility of a private language, but, Fogelin thinks, it establishes two important points: '(i) the construction of a private language may seem unproblematic only because we illicitly help ourselves to the logical features of expressions that occur in everyday language' (1976, 161; 1987, 174); '(ii) ... if we do give a symbol a public employment sufficient to fix its sense, then it is already up to the mark as far as significance goes, and there is no point in saying that it also has a private reference' (1976, 161; 1987, 175). The former point is central to PI §258 (see Section 11). I return to the latter point in Section 12.

A fourth argument, thinks Fogelin, shows 'the contingent impossibility of a private language' (1987, 175). The 'training argument' (1987, 175) contends that following a rule amounts to behaving as one has been trained to. Fogelin invokes the remark that Kripke assiduously avoids: 'there is a way of grasping a rule which is *not* an interpretation, but which, from case to case of application, is exhibited in what we call "following the rule" and "going against it"' (PI §201). Training constitutes a sceptical solution to the paradox about rule-following because it allows that any number of rules can fit any finite series of behaviour, while observing that we do not *accept* certain responses to our instructions to follow a particular rule as conforming to that rule. Someone who continues a series in response to the command to add 2, by writing, '... 1000, 1004, 1008, 1012 ...' will be held not to have followed the rule, even though there is *no justification* for saying this. Whoever learns arithmetic is trained to respond in certain ways, and 'that is the end of the matter' (Fogelin 1987, 176).

However, it is a contingent fact about human beings that there are no 'untrained trainer[s]' (1976, 164; 1987, 176), 'no linguistic self-starters' (1976, 165; 1987, 178). So I could not develop a private sensation-language because I could not be trained in the use of its terms by someone already familiar with their application, and I could not train myself without prior expertise. This does not make a private sensation-language *logically* impossible, but 'very general facts of nature' (PPF xii §365) exclude such possibilities.

Fogelin's reading differs from Kripke's, but it, too, attributes to Wittgenstein a scepticism about the determinacy of rule-following that admits of only a sceptical solution, wherein 'an unjustified (indeed, unjustifiable) belief is grounded in nothing more than a brute fact of human nature' (1987, 175). This reading, like Kripke's, is flawed, but it retains two significant virtues: (i) it suggests that there is no such thing as *the* private language argument but, rather, a network of intertwined considerations about problems raised by the idea of a private language; (ii) it emphasises the great importance for the diary-example of Wittgenstein's remarks about 'stage-setting' at PI §257. Both ideas have since furthered our understanding of Wittgenstein's investigations into private language.

11 The Fourth Wave: Stage-Setting

Counting waves eventually becomes a mug's game, but we can usefully identify one more. While many philosophers rode the Kripkean surf, other currents stirred in the depths. Many serious readers of Wittgenstein were dissatisfied with existing treatments of his later work, and this dissatisfaction yielded various re-evaluations of the passages on private language that characterise what I risk calling the Fourth Wave.[82] I start with Stewart Candlish – whose views are closer to Kenny and Hacker's than he allows.

Candlish (1980) criticises the 'Old Orthodoxy' (Fogelin's 'Public Check' argument) and the 'New Guardians' (Kenny and Hacker) for focusing too narrowly on PI §§258 and 265, and for neglecting the roles of other passages on private language. He agrees with Kenny and Hacker that the diary-example

---

[82] Some re-evaluations were surprising. Hintikka and Hintikka (1986) attribute to Wittgenstein a 'metaphysical Cartesianism' according to which, 'there really [are] private event-like experiences, including pains and other such sensations' (1986, 265). Wittgenstein, they think, rejects 'Cartesian semantics, not Cartesian metaphysics' (1986, 250). Cook (1994) argues that Wittgenstein endorsed phenomenalism from 1929 through the *Investigations*. Jacquette (1997, 274–297) thinks that, for Wittgenstein, sensations are private objects, particular tokens of which cannot be named, but types of which can be described. All these approaches misinterpret Wittgenstein's transitional writings and carry those misinterpretations into the *Investigations*. See Hymers 2017, 26–73. See also Pears 1988, 199–327; Stern 1995; Gert 2000, 100–101.

presents a semantic challenge about how a term in a private language could be given any meaning. However, he thinks that Kenny's reading faces as much difficulty as the Old Orthodoxy.

On Kenny's reading, Wittgenstein's reasoning is 'wildly fallacious', says Candlish (1980, 94). Kenny imagines confronting the private speaker after the attempted definition of 'S' by private ostension and asking what 'S' means. The diarist could say, 'By "S" I mean the sensation I named "S" in the past' (Kenny 1973, 194), but this would require justification by a memory of the correlation of a past sensation with a past application of 'S'. Kenny reiterates the complaint with this procedure:

> But of course he must call up the *right* memory. Now is it possible that the wrong memory might come at this call? If not, then 'S' means whatever memory occurs to him in connection with 'S', and again whatever seems right is right. If so, then he does not really know what he means. (1973, 194)

Candlish reads this as a dilemma: if the wrong memory *cannot* be called up, then 'S' is meaningless because it cannot be misapplied–no rule has been given. If the wrong memory *can* be called up, then the private speaker 'does not really know what he means' (194). The latter horn, insists Candlish, unreasonably requires *infallibility* in subsequent applications of 'S', but I can understand how to use a term even if I sometimes misapply it (Candlish 1980, 91).[83]

However, when Kenny writes, 'If so, then he does not really know what he means', he is *not* completing a dilemma.[84] He is saying, '*If it is so–that whatever seems right is right*–then he does not really know what he means.' That is just what we should expect, if 'attaching meaning to a name does not mean acquiring infallibility in its use' (Kenny 1973, 193). So Kenny has not assumed that 'there *is* actually an application of a sign to a sensation by a private-language user, and that the problem is one of later remembering this earlier application' (Candlish 1980, 91). Kenny's point is Candlish's: *there has been no successful definition of 'S', and no rule has been established for the application of 'S'.*

Charles Dunlop, following Candlish, complains further that Kenny and Hacker have overlooked the crucial importance of Wittgenstein's discussion at PI §§27–36 of ostensive definition (1984, 364n4–365n4).[85] In fact, both Kenny (1973, 182–183) and Hacker (1972, 235) indicate that these remarks

---

[83] See Candlish 2011 [1998], 120; Candlish and Wrisley 2019, §3.4.
[84] For the same error see Marks 1975, 154–155; Law 2004, 173; Wrisley 2011, 490–492; Lin 2017, 261. Kenny's text *is* ambiguous, but his summary (1973, 15) confirms my claim.
[85] See Marks 1975, 167.

are significant for the critique of private language. However, beginning with the Fourth Wave, they come clearly to the surface.

The main reason for emphasising the remarks on ostensive definition here lies in the passages immediately preceding the diary-example. One of the tasks of PI §§244–256 (see Section 6) is to undermine the supposition that our *ordinary* sensation-terms refer to superprivate objects. However, a question remains about whether such a private sensation-language might yet be *possible*:

> – But suppose I didn't have any natural expression of sensation, but only had sensations? And now I simply *associate* names with sensations, and use these names in descriptions. – (PI §256)

How could one acquire a grasp of sensation-terms if this were the case? Here we encounter the child-genius:

> 'What would it be like if human beings showed no outward signs of pain (did not groan, grimace, etc.)? Then it would be impossible to teach a child the use of the word "tooth-ache".' – Well, let's assume the child is a genius and itself invents a name for the sensation! – But then, of course, he couldn't make himself understood when he used the word. – So does he understand the name, without being able to explain its meaning to anyone? – But what does it mean to say that he has 'named his pain'? – How has he done this naming of pain?! And whatever he did, what was its purpose? – When one says 'He gave a name to his sensation' one forgets that a great deal of stage-setting in the language is presupposed if the mere act of naming is to make sense. And when we speak of someone's having given a name to pain, what is presupposed is the existence of the grammar of the word 'pain'; it shows the post where the new word is stationed. (PI §257)[86]

This 'stage-setting' argument was noted by Candlish (1980, 86), Hallett (1977, 337–339), Fogelin (1976, 159–162; 1987, 172–175), Cook (1972, 62, 65), Goldberg (1971, 88) and even earlier by Holborow (1967, 350),[87] but it gets its due only with Stroud (2002 [1983]) and Williams (1983).[88]

As we saw (Section 3), the argument appears in the *Big Typescript*, immediately after a discussion of 'the great variety of language-games' (BT 209). There the stage-setting – what has 'been prepared in advance' (BT 209 v) – is found in Wittgenstein's discussion of ostensive definition at BT 31–33.[89] In *PI*, immediately

---

[86] The German does not use the 'stage-setting' metaphor, but the argument has become known by this name, so I quote Anscombe's translation.

[87] See also Hardin 1959, 518; Manser 1969, 169–171.

[88] The argument has since been stressed by Hacker 2019a [1990], 73–78; Johnston 1993, 17–18; Stern 1994, 560, 1995, 182–186; Glock 1996, 312–313; McGinn 2013 [1997], 152–158; Canfield 2001; Stern 2004, 185; Tanesini 2004, 102; Fogelin 2009, 70–71; Wrisley 2011; Hymers 2017, 62–67.

[89] Other proposals for stage-setting include: Teaching 'new pain-behaviour' (PI §244) (Donagan 1966, 342; Rembert 1975, 238); 'a human childhood' (Cook 1972, 65); 'pre-existing physical

following an examination of 'the variety of language-games' (PI §23), we find a parallel discussion of ostensive definition that suggests, first, that we distinguish ostensive *teaching* and *learning* from ostensive *definition*.[90] The former is important in the acquisition of language, but the latter presupposes a grasp of language. Second, ostensive teaching and learning rely extensively on features of context, including, eventually, linguistic context, to *disambiguate* ostension. When I point towards a book before us, the gesture alone does not determine whether I point to the book, its shape, its size, its colour, the image on its cover, the number of books present, and so on. If I share a language with you, then I can specify: 'Is this your book?' 'Like most books, this is roughly a parallelepiped.' 'I'm colour-blind: is this green?' 'Who's that on the cover?' If I cannot rely on such disambiguations, then I might resort to comparisons and contrasts with other things to make it clear what I am pointing at – for example, by grouping the book together with other books or other green things or other parallelepipeds, and so on, but this is gradually to fall back on ostensive *teaching*.

The lesson for §257 is that it is unclear how the child, however ingenious, can name private sensations, which admit of no such disambiguation – disambiguation from concurrent sensations, or from their location, duration, intensity, and so on. Concentrate on your unnamed sensation. –Now on the intensity of that sensation. –Now on its location. –Now on its duration. What did you do differently each time? How could you do it without the concepts needed to distinguish a sensation from its intensity, duration or location? The challenge is to show how disambiguation can be achieved without this stage-setting.

These themes recur in the diary-example. Barry Stroud gives a clear and direct statement:

> [T]here is nothing new in Wittgenstein's later concentration ... in *PI* §258 on the attempt to 'associate' a name and a thing by pointing to or fixing one's attention on the thing. We are simply being reminded, in a more concrete and graphic way, of the real force of that earlier point [at PI §§27–36]. What is new here is the idea that the naming of the sensation is supposed to take place in a language only the speaker can understand. (2002 [1983], 74)

> [O]nce all the normal 'stage-setting' or 'grammar' of sensation-words is excluded from the situation, as it must be in order to 'name the sensation' in the required special way, the original naked ceremony of pointing or concentrating one's attention does not manage to determine *anything* as the correct use of the sign 'S'. There is no 'criterion' of correctness in the

---

connections of pain' (Pears 1988, 396); ordinary practical abilities of speakers (Schulte 1992, 144–145); 'shared activities in a public social world' (Maslin 2001, 223); 'agreement in judgments' (PI §242) (Kanterian 2017, 448).

[90] Law (2004, 172–173) misses the importance of this distinction.

sense that there is nothing in what happens in the ceremony so far that brings it about that some particular application of the term is correct and that some other is not. (75)[91]

Consequently, says Stroud, 'there is so far nothing that even an infallible memory could remember' (75).[92]

Meredith Williams emphasises similar themes. Commentators have focused erroneously, she says, on the '*Consistency Assumption*': the terms of a private language must refer to objects 'of the same kind as the object originally baptised' (1983, 59) if they are to be meaningful. The proper focus belongs on the '*Naming Assumption*' (58): sensation-terms get their meaning from the 'ostensive baptism of a sensory experience' (58–59). This assumption is undermined by Wittgenstein's discussion of ostensive definition at PI §§27–36, to which he adverts at PI §257. The role of the diary-example, says Williams, is to show that the Consistency Assumption cannot be satisfied by a private language because 'no standard for subsequent namings has been set . . . ' (65).[93]

There is good reason to emphasise stage-setting in the case of the child-genius, and we might plausibly agree with Stroud and Stern (2004, 184–185) that the diary-example makes the same point in a vivid way, but Canfield thinks this reading involves a circularity. The last four lines of PI §258, he suggests, are 'supposed to demonstrate the failure of the would-be private ostensive definition' (2001, 383), and a premise in the argument for that conclusion is that 'I have no criterion of correctness' (PI §258). However, on the no-stage-setting reading, the reason that I have no criterion of correctness for my use of 'S' is that no ostensive definition has been given – which was to be *shown*. Canfield concludes that PI §258 must add some 'new point' to the child-genius example, and he argues that '§257 says that setting up a rule requires a practice, whereas §258 (like §202) says that following a rule requires a practice' (393).

Defenders of the no-stage-setting reading of the diary-example can deny Canfield's assumption that the last four lines of PI §258 are 'supposed to demonstrate the failure of the would-be private ostensive definition' (2001, 383). '[T]he narrator's closing words are best read as providing a forceful restatement of the case for thinking that the interlocutor has done nothing that amounts to giving a word a meaning' (Stern 2004, 185).[94] However, these lines

---

[91] So a criterion is not a 'method' (Wright 2001, 300) for appraising my spontaneous judgments about my sensations.
[92] *If* I could pick out S, Lin (2017, 264) contends, then I could establish a private language in the 'short duration', but this antecedent begs the question.
[93] See Dunlop 1984, 351; Dancy 1985, 77–78; Gert 1986, 419. Sauvé (1988) considers the stage-setting argument but reads PI §258 with Malcolm.
[94] See Wrisley 2011, 493.

do seem to be critical of the proposal that 'I commit to memory the connection between the sign and the sensation' by concentrating my attention. If that critique says only that there is no reason to think that a definition of 'S' has been given because the usual stage-setting for naming is absent, then it begs the question by ignoring this proposal.

One plausible response is that concentrating my attention depends as much on stage-setting as naming does (see PI §§33–34; Stroud 2002 [1983], 75). Like the object of one's pointing, the object of one's attention is determined by the circumstances: 'Just as making a move in chess doesn't consist only in pushing a piece from here to there on the board – nor yet in the thoughts and feelings that accompany the move: but in the circumstances that we call "playing a game of chess", "solving a chess problem", and the like' (PI §33). Attending requires as much disambiguation as does pointing, so it cannot circumvent the challenges to private ostensive definition.

However, perhaps we can reconcile Canfield's claim (that the last four lines of the diary-example make an additional point)[95] with the stage-setting interpretation in a way that also helps clarify the connection between PI §258 and PI §202– the passage celebrated by defenders of the community view. I suggested earlier (Section 5) that the advice of PI §202 might be to keep PI §201 in mind when we consider private language:

> [T]here is a way of grasping a rule which is *not* an interpretation, but which, from case to case of application, is exhibited in what we call 'following the rule' and 'going against it'. (PI §201)

This remark reminds us that, when we judge whether someone has learned a rule, '– The application is still a criterion of understanding' (PI §146). We have no higher court of appeal regarding someone's understanding than our ordinary judgments about how well she applies a rule, if at all. The teacher's judgment that a pupil can do addition is based entirely on the pupil's performance with actual sums.

In the diary-case there is no performance, no manifestation, even to myself (see Stern 1994, 559), of my understanding the rule for applying 'S'. I have a sensation, I 'focus' my attention, and I write 'S' in my diary. Later, I have a sensation, and I am to remember the connection – the rule – that I was to have established earlier. The problem is that the criterion for whether I have applied the ostensible rule for 'S' correctly or not is to be given by *the very application of 'S' that is to be assessed with reference to that criterion*, and this renders my judgment that I have understood my rule for 'S' trivial. It is as though the

---

[95] Canfield's own account (2001, 388) is baroque. See Wrisley 2011, 492–497 for a critique.

question of my understanding were settled by my *avowal* of understanding (*contra* PI §§151–152). So, given what *generally counts* as a criterion for someone's having understood how to apply the rule, there is no criterion: nothing logically distinguishes my being right from my thinking I am right.[96] Canfield is right, then, that the diary-example expands on the example of the child genius, but the new point is that *further elements* of the stage-setting for naming are also missing.

The subsequent passages reinforce the doubt that any naming of a sensation or fixing of a rule for the use of 'S' has taken place. At PI §260 we consider whether I might at least '*believe* that this is sensation S again.' '– Perhaps you *believe* that you believe it!' is the sarcastic response. If I have not defined 'S', then I cannot believe rightly or wrongly that S is recurring (Kenny 1973, 194), and '"S" so far has' no function. Nor, then, is it clear how I can 'inwardly *resolve* to use the word in such-and-such a way' (PI §262) for it is unclear how concentrating my attention on my feeling (PI §263) could establish a 'technique of applying the word' (PI §262). Without the appropriate stage-setting, I can no more give myself 'a private explanation of a word' than 'my right hand' can 'give my left hand money' (PI §268). Worse yet, the private diarist's aspiration to apply 'S' to a *sensation,* assumes too much, 'For "sensation" is a word of our common language, which is not a language intelligible only to me' (PI §261). It is implausible to think that what the private diarist wants to do can be described without employing terms that undermine the ostensible privacy of the diary.

PI §259 suggests that the mere *impression* of a rule could no more function as a rule than the impression of a balance could function as a balance, a theme pursued further in PI §267, where a contrast is drawn between imagining 'what is called justifying the choice of dimensions for a bridge' by 'imagining making loading tests' and actually 'justifying an imagined choice of dimensions' (PI §267). This distinction, in turn, is like that between 'look[ing] at a clock to see what time it is' and 'mov[ing] the hands of a clock till their position strikes me as right' (PI §266).[97] The timetable example of PI §265, central to Malcolm's and Kenny's readings, sounds a similar note: 'Looking up a table in the imagination is no more looking up a table than the image of the result of an imagined experiment is the result of an experiment' (PI §265).

The Fourth Wave's interpretation of the diary-example in light of the case of the child-genius and the earlier passages on ostensive definition is a significant

---

[96] Baker and Hacker (1984, 13–14) hint at this point. Compare: An utterance can be mistaken only if we can 'distinguish the criterion for the content of an utterance from the criterion for its truth' (Kenny 1966, 368). This is not a matter of *verifiability* or of what I can *know* but of what, paradigmatically, *constitutes* understanding a rule – its application in actual cases.

[97] For a less satisfactory reading see Hymers 1997.

advance. It helps dislodge the diary-example from its traditionally central place in the critique of private language and lets us see that there are many different arguments employed in that critique. If any theme unifies these arguments, it is doubt that sensations are analogous to objects in physical space.

None of this aims to show that a private language is *impossible*. Rather it leaves defenders of private language with a question: given what ordinarily counts as pointing at something, attending to something, naming something, following a rule – why think that concentrating on my sensation is sufficient to give it a name?

12 The Human Manometer

At PI §270 we return to the diary of PI §258, with a twist:

> Let us now imagine a use for the entry of the sign 'S' in my diary. I find out the following from my experience: whenever I have a particular sensation, a manometer shows that my blood pressure is rising. This puts me in a position to report that my blood pressure is rising without using any apparatus. This is a useful result. And now it seems quite indifferent whether I've recognized the sensation *correctly* or not. Suppose that I regularly make a mistake in identifying it, this does not make any difference at all. And this alone shows that the supposition of this mistake was merely sham. (We, as it were, turned a knob which looked as if it could be used to adjust something in the machine; but it was a mere ornament not connected with the mechanism at all.)
>
> And what reason do we have here for calling 'S' the name of a sensation? Perhaps the kind of way this sign is employed in this language-game. – And why a 'particular sensation': that is, the same one every time? Well, we're supposing, aren't we, that we write 'S' every time. (PI §270)

I argue that we should read this passage in light of Wittgenstein's treatment of the problem of the inverted spectrum (Section 12.1). It is an argument for thinking that the uses of sensation-terms do not depend on any prior identification of sensations, *even if we think of sensations as superprivate objects*. Reaching this conclusion, however, requires a detour through the existing literature.

The manometer example has inspired significant misunderstandings. Ayer (1954, 67), for example, likened it to the way in which one's sensation-terms are 'tied up with [one's] natural expressions of sensation' (PI §256), as though the manometer readings were natural expressions of S,[98] but the two cases differ. My natural expression of a sensation is what Wittgenstein elsewhere (e.g., BBB,

---

[98] See Tanburn 1963, 95; Hallett 1977, 347; Hintikka and Hintikka 1986, 263–264.

24–25; see Hertzberg 2023) calls a *criterion* that justifies others' judgments that I am in pain. On one influential reading (Lycan 1971; Baker 1974), a criterion for my pain gives others *necessary evidence* that I am in pain. Ordinary evidence is evidence only against background assumptions: a rash on my palms is evidence of my allergy to penicillin only given modern immunology. Without the concepts of immunoglobin, antibodies and histamines, I simply have red, itchy palms. By contrast, my cries and grimaces, on this understanding of 'criterion', remain evidence of my pain in *any* context – although other evidence (e.g., my being an actor on stage) can override their evidentiary value. According to another view (Malcolm 1954, 543–547; Canfield 1981; McDowell 1982), criteria *define* concepts in the sense that if a criterion for my pain is satisfied (as when I cry out after an anvil falls on my foot), then I *am* in pain. (The actor's behaviour on stage only *seems* to satisfy a criterion for pain.) The rash on my palms does not similarly guarantee my allergy to penicillin.

My hypertension is like the rash on my hands, not like my spontaneous cries of pain, whichever way we understand 'criterion'. It does not *express* my sensation S. The connection between S and my increased blood-pressure is 'just a contingent fact that happened to be discovered' (Holborow 1967, 351). The manometer readings may thus be *evidence* for others of my having S, but not a criterion for my having S.

As importantly, evidence and criteria are evidence and criteria for *others*, not for me, as the asymmetry between first- and other-person uses of sensation-vocabulary suggests (see Section 6.3). I need neither in order sincerely to express my sensations, verbally or nonverbally. I do not *discover* that I have S by consulting the manometer. On the other hand, once I note the correlation between my sensation and the manometer-readings, my having S becomes *evidence* for me of my *hypertension*, and my writing 'S' in my diary becomes evidence for others of this same condition and a criterion for them of my having S again.[99]

Another early misunderstanding read Wittgenstein as arguing that sensations are *irrelevant* to the meanings of sensation-terms.[100] This interpretation

---

[99] See Hanfling 1984, 476; Mulhall 2007, 131; Hacker 2019b [1990], 73–75. Lin (2021, 155) and Fan (2021, 52) muddy these waters. Hacker (2019b [1990], 72) correctly takes the example to correlate my *having S* and my having hypertension. Kenny (1973, 194), Clegg (1974, 212), Fogelin (1987, 174), Hunter (1985, 85) and Johnston (1993, 21) all correlate my *use of 'S'* with my hypertension. Cook (1994, 321) thinks the correlation is between the manometer readings and my diary-entries.

[100] See Wellman 1959, 229; Todd 1962, 217; Tanburn 1963, 95–96; Kultgen 1968, 37; and, later, Cook 1994, 327. Papineau (2011, 181–182) teeters between this reading and Kenny's (discussed next in this section).

assumes that sensations are private objects and concludes that *if* the use of 'S' to report hypertension does not require recognising my private sensation, then sensations are 'no longer important' (Todd 1962, 217) to the meanings of sensation-terms. Strawson (1954, 84) draws a similar conclusion from the beetle-in-a-box of PI §293. However, what is in question is whether I must *identify* my sensations – like faces in an old photograph – if I am to express them linguistically. 'If my use of a sensation-word satisfies the normal outward criteria and if I truthfully declare that I have that sensation, then I *have* it – there is not a further problem of my applying the word right or wrong within myself' (Malcolm 1954, 556).

The need to identify my sensations arose from construing first-person authority as privileged access (Section 6.3). And something like Malcolm's point – that the manometer example concerns the irrelevance for the meanings of sensation-terms of my identifying my sensations – is widely affirmed.[101] This consensus, however, masks disagreement about *why* the supposition that I make a mistake is 'merely sham' (PI §270).[102]

On one popular reading, the manometer example correlates the alleged private sensation, S, with a publicly observable phenomenon, an increase in my blood-pressure. This might provide the criterion of correctness missing from the diary-example of PI §258: circumstances in which 'S' is correctly applied (when my blood-pressure rises) and others in which it is incorrectly applied (when my blood-pressure does not rise). If 'S' then has a public use but includes a private connection with S, then a private component of meaning has been preserved for sensation-terms. However, the effect of this public correlate is to render the meaning of 'S' public. So no private language has been established after all.

Kenny (1973, 194–195) is the best-known proponent of the argument so sketched.[103] On his reading, PI §270 argues that '"S" is not the name of a private object' (Kenny 1973, 195) *because* misidentifying S would not matter to the application of 'S', and it would not matter because I would have no reason 'to say that I have misidentified the sensation rather than misremembered which

---

[101] See Cooke 1974, 48; Hopkins 1974, 138; Senchuk 1976, 237; Bouveresse 1987 [1976], 542–544; Hacker 2019b [1990], 73; Canfield 1991, 132; Johnston 1993, 21; Glock 1996, 314; McGinn 2013 [1997], 165–166; Nielsen 2008, 165; Fogelin 2009, 74; McDougall 2013, 61–63.

[102] Wilson (1998) suggests it does not *matter* whether I misidentify S 'because the manometer reading always, or almost always, takes precedence' (1998, 15) – but then the results are *not useful*.

[103] See also Garver 1960, 395–396; Shoemaker 1966, 358; Kultgen 1968, 37; Cook 1972, 51–52; Bloor 1983, 60–61; Candlish 1980, 93; Gert 1986, 428–431; Fogelin 1987, 174; McGinn 2013 [1997], 165–166; Schroeder 2006, 216.

kind of sensation goes with the rise' (195) in blood-pressure (see Fogelin 1987, 174).

However, this argument begs the question. Consider a parallel example:

> Suppose that I correlate traffic lights with the movement of traffic that I cannot observe directly. Whenever I see a green light, a traffic camera shows that the traffic is moving. So I can say that the traffic is moving without using the traffic camera – a useful result. And now it seems quite indifferent whether I have recognised the light right or not. So the hypothesis that I make a mistake is mere show.

It is mysterious *how* I could be right about the movement of traffic with better than an even chance if my getting the colour of the light correct is irrelevant.[104] Likewise, it would not matter whether I had identified the sensation correctly or not, only if it had *already* been shown that *no such act of identification was necessary* to make 'S' the name of a sensation.

On Hacker's reading, by contrast, the publicity of the sign 'S' is not the *conclusion* of the passage but a *reason* for thinking that the meanings of sensation-terms do not require (re)identifying sensations.[105] Rather than argue that the use of 'S' is public because no need for identification arises, PI §270 argues that no need for identification arises because the use of 'S' is public.[106] This view is supported by earlier drafts of the example, in which the sensation correlated with the manometer-readings is *pain* (MS 165, 146–148) and not the recurrent private object of PI §258 (see Hacker 2019b [1990], 74–75).

However, if S is not a private object, then the contention that it does not matter whether I misidentify it is puzzling. Why allow that an ordinary sensation might be misidentified, only to insist that it would not matter if it were, if ordinary sensations cannot be identified or misidentified in advance of their expression? If the fact that ordinary first-person uses of sensation-terms do not presuppose the application of criteria is insufficient to show that my use of 'S' does not require first identifying S, adding that the misidentification of S would be irrelevant to using 'S' to indicate hypertension will not help. As Stephen Mulhall observes, 'Anyone who thinks that misrecognition of sensations is possible will ... take it that the threat of misrecognizing the sensation will in fact undermine the usefulness of the correlation' (2007, 125) – the same objection faced by Kenny's reading.

---

[104] See Hunter 1985, 84–85; Pears 2006, 57, 59. Bloor (1983, 61) makes a related complaint but takes ordinary, first-person uses of sensation-terms to rest on prior acts of identification.
[105] See Diamond 2000, 276.
[106] See also Canfield 1991, 132; Glock 1996, 314; McGinn 2013 [1997], 165–166; McDougall 2013, 61–63.

Perhaps there is a purposeful ambiguity in how to understand *S* – as a private object or as an ordinary sensation.[107] We might take Wittgenstein's view to be that in *either case* identification plays no role in giving 'S' meaning. If S is an ordinary sensation, then the meaning of 'S' rests on no identification because the paradigmatic function of 'S' is to express my sensation. If S is a private object, then, again, the meaning of 'S' rests on no identification, for different reasons.

But what reasons? How is Wittgenstein not begging the question against the prospective private speaker? I do not see how to relieve this worry without going beyond PI §270, but we need not go *too far* afield for an answer.

12.1 The Inverted Spectrum

The supposition that I make a mistake is 'merely sham' (PI §270) because the prospective private speaker is committed to saying so by parity of reasoning with the case of the inverted spectrum:

> The essential thing about private experience is really not that each person possesses his own specimen, but that nobody knows whether other people also have *this* or something else. The assumption would thus be possible– though unverifiable–that one section of mankind had one visual impression of red, and another section another. (PI §272)

Don't be distracted by the word 'unverifiable'! Wittgenstein's point is that the only reason I could have for thinking that someone's impression of red differed from mine lies in differences in our responses to coloured objects, and the inverted-spectrum hypothesis removes exactly those differences in response. So the proponent of private language must allow that we could agree in all our colour-judgments, while having different colour-impressions – and also that we could agree in our uses of sensation-vocabulary while having different 'private sensations':

> 'Imagine a person who could not remember *what* the word "pain" meant – so that he constantly called different things by that name – but nevertheless used it in accordance with the usual symptoms and presuppositions of pain' – in short, he uses it as we all do. Here I'd like to say: a wheel that can be turned though nothing else moves with it is not part of the mechanism. (PI §271)

These 'different things' would be private objects. They could not be ordinary sensations if I use the word 'pain' as English-speakers ordinarily do.

---

[107] Canfield hints: 'The use [of "S"] will have shifted, from private to public' (1991, 132).

In lecture-notes from the mid-1930s, Wittgenstein complains that the apparent intelligibility of the inverted-spectrum hypothesis rests on severing attributions of colour-perception to observers from the behavioural criteria on which those attributions normally rest.

> It is clear that we ... use the words 'seeing red' in such a way that we can say 'he /A/ sees red but doesn't show it'; on the other hand it is easy to see that we would have no use for these words if their application was severed from the criteria of behaviour. (LPE 233)

Ordinarily, I say that someone sees something different from what I see because she says so – or because she responds differently to the thing in question (LPE 230). Such differences emerge most noticeably in cases of colour-blindness, but there is evidence that people with statistically normal colour-vision may disagree subtly in their colour-judgments (Neitz and Jacobs 1986). These subtle differences may tempt us to think that inverted spectra – cases of *undetectable* differences in colour-perception – are possible. 'It seems, if once we have admitted that it can happen under peculiar circumstances, that it may always happen' (LPE 285). However, this is like thinking that if one coin can be counterfeit, then *all* coins might be counterfeit. '[I]t is clear that the very idea of seeing red loses its use if we can never know if the other does not see something utterly different' (LPE 285).

In the case of the inverted spectrum, differences in verbal and non-verbal behaviour – the only reasons we have for suspecting that someone sees something differently – are imagined absent. The application of colour-terms in our attributions of experiences to others is thus severed from the ordinary behavioural criteria for such attributions, and the defender of the inverted-spectrum hypothesis happily agrees that our colour-judgments may converge even while we 'see' different things. In that case, the supposedly private colour-impression plays no role in our employment of colour-terms. However, if the private-language advocate allows this, then *by parity of reasoning* the same allowance should apply to all supposedly private sensations. So when the usual behavioural criteria for attributions to others of sensations like pain are suspended, as in the diary-example, it follows that we might agree in our use of ordinary terms like 'pain' without sharing the private sensation. But if it does not matter what private sensation accompanies our use of the word 'pain', then it does not matter for the use of 'pain' whether that sensation has been correctly identified. The word 'pain' functions in complete independence of the private object. That is why 'the supposition of this mistake was merely sham' (PI §270).

The argument presupposes an unstated premise: *if my impression of red or my sensation of pain can be undetectably different from yours, then my impression of red or my sensation of pain can be undetectably different from one occasion to the next*. However, the private speaker might object that, although private objects play no role in public meanings, we can *converge* in our public uses of sensation-terms *because* we have these private meanings (or referents). It does not matter that we have different private sensations, but it *does* matter that *I* have the *same* private sensation whenever I say that my knee hurts. Although we cannot detect differences in each other's private sensations and colour-impressions, I *can* detect differences in my own from occasion to occasion: I can *recognise* them – reidentify them – remember them! So 'When I say 'I am in pain', I am at any rate justified *before myself*' (PI §289).

Wittgenstein has already short-circuited this objection in his discussions of the child-genius (PI §257) and the diary-example (PI §258). We had no reason to think that either the child-genius or the private diarist assigned a name to private sensations because there was no way to disambiguate inner ostensive definition – no way to say that one inwardly points or attends to one sensation, rather than a concurrent one, or to a sensation and not its duration, or location, or intensity, and so on. So the analogy between undetectable, *inter*subjective differences in private sensations or colour-impressions and undetectable, *intra*-subjective differences in private sensations or colour-impressions holds fast, and, with it, the argument for thinking that the alleged identification of my supposed private sensation in the manometer example is irrelevant to my use of 'S'.

Wittgenstein does not connect the inverted spectrum and the manometer until PI §288 and not as explicitly as he might. However, other questions about the inverted spectrum need answering first. The idea that my colour-terms retain, in addition to their public meaning, a private meaning or reference, known only to me, is the theme of PI §§273–277:

> What about the word 'red'? – Am I to say that it signifies something 'confronting us all', and that everyone should really have another word, besides this one, to signify his *own* impression of red? Or is it like this: the word 'red' signifies something known to us all; and in addition, for each person, it signifies something known only to him? (Or perhaps, rather: it *refers* to something known only to him.) (PI §273)

Wittgenstein deals first with private reference. Saying that the word 'red' on my lips privately refers to my colour-impression expresses 'a particular experience in doing philosophy' (§274), but it says nothing about the word's function (cf. Schulte 2011, 445). This point goes back to PI §13 and is reinforced by the critique of private ostensive definition at PI §§257–258. Moreover, the so-called *transparency of perception* suggests that we do not *really* think that colour-terms refer to something private when we are not engaged in philosophical reflection:

> Look at the blue of the sky and say to yourself, 'How blue the sky is!' – When you do it spontaneously – without philosophical purposes – the idea never crosses your mind that this impression of colour belongs only to *you*. (PI §275)

When you make such an exclamation, you do not try to point within yourself but at the sky.

Talk of private signification is no better. The temptation to think that I mean something private by my colour-terms, suggests Wittgenstein, is the result of a particular way of *attending* to colours: '... I immerse myself in the colour ... ' (PI §277). I attend to it for its own sake, as if I had 'detached the colour *impression* from the object, like a membrane' (PI §276). The experience is like attending to my visual impression of a square table, viewed from an angle, and learning to represent it by drawing a trapezoid. This is philosophically innocuous in a drawing class, but in the imaginations of philosophers of perception it becomes an argument for sense-data, as we are misled by the analogy between physical space and phenomenal space. Just as there are objects in physical space, we want to say, there are objects in phenomenal space, and our immediate apprehension of them accounts for our mediate perception of objects in physical space. The same applies to the colours of objects in physical space. When I learn to represent the colours of an object in a painting, I may imaginatively detach the colours from the object and attend to variations in shading, illumination, texture and saturation. Again, this is philosophically innocuous in a painting class, but when the philosopher of perception takes brush in hand, the resulting colour-patch in phenomenal space acquires the properties of an object in physical space – one that only the philosopher can 'see.'

The philosopher may then say, '"I know how the colour green looks to *me"* – surely that makes sense!' (PI §278), and such a sentence might be intelligibly uttered in *some* context. '– Certainly; what use of the sentence are you thinking of?' (PI §278). 'I don't know how the colour green looks to you,' I say, criticising your choice of hues, 'but I know how it looks to *me*!' And I paint over what you have just done. "Je sais comment *m*'apparait la couleur verte. '[C]'est instable, parfois dangereux'" (Pastoureau and Simonet 2014, 66). But no such context has been given, and what makes sense in a painting class now floats free from the moorings of intelligibility. With nothing against which to calibrate 'how the colour green looks to me', the expression loses its sense, like an attempt to measure something in visual space (see Section 3). Wittgenstein parodies the result: 'Imagine someone saying, "But I know how tall I am!" and laying his hand on top of his head to indicate it!' (PI §279).

The temptation to model phenomenal space on physical space reappears at PI §280, where we imagine painting a picture of a prospective stage set. We may want to say that the painting is a double representation of the set to be built and of the artist's private impression of how the stage should look – but that it can be the latter only for the artist. However, '[W]hat right have I to speak in this second case of a representation or piece of information – if these words were correctly used in the *first* case?' (PI §280). We forget that phenomenal space and physical space have different properties. 'Representation' can no more mean the same thing in phenomenal space and physical space than 'same length' can (Section 3). A parallel point applies to colour-vocabulary and sensation-vocabulary alike. It is thinking of colour-impressions or of sensations as private objects that makes it seem that we refer to them as we would to public objects.

Severing attributions of colour-perceptions to others from the behavioural criteria on which we base those attributions made the inverted spectrum seem intelligible. By parity of reasoning, I argued, the identification of an ostensibly private sensation would be irrelevant to the use of the corresponding sensation-term. Wittgenstein rejoins the discussion of pain and behavioural criteria at PI §281:

> 'But doesn't what you say amount to this: that there is no pain, for example, without *pain-behaviour*?' – It amounts to this: that only of a living human being and what resembles (behaves like) a living human being can one say: it has sensations; it sees; is blind; hears; is deaf; is conscious or unconscious. (PI §281)

PI §§282–288 explore the relation between bodily behaviour and the concepts of sensation and of pain, attempting to clarify this thought, eventually returning to the idea that if we sever the use of sensation-vocabulary from behaviour, then I can be mistaken about my own sensations (PI §288). But the path is rocky.

We sometimes attribute pain to inanimate objects, such as dolls, 'But this use of the concept of pain is a secondary one' (PI §282), and although we might say that 'in a fairy tale a pot too can see and hear' (PI §282), it is not clear that this makes sense – nor, indeed, that fairy tales *must* make sense.

So much for obvious exceptions. PI §283 then asks, 'What gives us *so much as the idea* that beings, things, can feel?' and near the end of the passage we hear an echo of PI §281: 'Only of what behaves like a human being can one say that it *has* pains' (PI §283). But other thoughts crowd in. Do I conclude that others have sensations by analogy with my own case? That would require me to *recognise* my sensations – as the manometer example suggests I do *not* – while using words like 'pain' as others do. And why not attribute sensations to stones or plants? Could I turn to stone while continuing to suffer pain? Could a stone have pains? Could a stone have a mind? Can a mind have pains? Can a body *have* a mind? Can a body have pains?

The ensuing passages revisit some of these questions. Neither my body nor my hand has pains, but *I* have pain in my body or in my hand.[108] This is made 'clear' by the fact that 'if someone has a pain in his hand, then the *hand* does not say so (unless it writes it), and one does not comfort the hand, but the sufferer: one looks into his eyes' (PI §286). Why do we do this? 'How am I filled with pity *for this human being*? How does it come out what the object of my pity is?' (PI §287). We get no immediate answers to *these* questions, but we might think of what Wittgenstein calls 'natural' (PI §185) or 'primitive' reactions (PPF xi §289). Our responses to the suffering of others are part of 'the natural history of human beings' (PI §415), not the result of a fragile induction from our own case.[109]

The importance of these natural reactions becomes vivid when we consider how we recognise and describe facial expressions. Doing so 'does not consist in giving the measurements of the face!' (PI §285). We describe faces as happy, sorrowful, angry, friendly, trustworthy or not, worried – and, if we are sighted, we do this as surely as we grasp any of these concepts. Our language-games of facial description are rooted in our primitive reactions to the faces of our fellows. 'Think, too, how one can imitate a man's face without seeing one's own in a mirror' (PI §285).

These primitive reactions are also manifested in the fact that 'Our attitude to what is alive and to what is dead is not the same. All our reactions are different' (PI §284). And if 'a corpse seems to us quite inaccessible to pain' (PI §284), then how much more so a stone?

> Look at a stone and imagine it having sensations. – One says to oneself: How could one so much as get the idea of ascribing a *sensation to a thing*? One might as well ascribe it to a number! – And now look at a wriggling fly, and at once these difficulties vanish, and pain seems able to get a *foothold* here, where before everything was, so to speak, too *smooth* for it. (PI §284)

A corpse manifests no behaviour that would warrant applying sensation-predicates to it, but perhaps a wriggling fly does. Its behaviour is like that of a human being in the relevant sense.

---

[108] This does not mean that a *mind* has pains in a body but that 'the person who is suffering is the person who manifests pain' (PI §302).
[109] See Tang 2015, 118–120.

This detour through facial expressions, wriggling flies, stones and corpses reminds us that the conviction that another is in pain is linked, through primitive, natural reactions, to the other's behaviour.

> Here it is a help to remember that it is a primitive reaction to take care of, to treat, the place that hurts when someone else is in pain, and not merely when one is so oneself – hence it is a primitive reaction to attend to the pain-behaviour of another, as, also, *not* to attend to one's own pain-behaviour. (RPP I §915)

So trying to imagine that a stone has pain, or that I might turn to stone while still having pain involves fundamentally altering the normal stage-setting for our uses of sensation-terms. It severs the connection between behaviour and our uses of sensation-terms in the way imagined in the diary-example. This is the focus of PI §288.

We might yet want to say that I could 'turn to stone [while] my pain goes on' (PI §288), but Wittgenstein's response here recalls PI §270: '– What if I were mistaken, and it was no longer *pain*?' (PI §288). We may want to reply, '– But surely I can't be mistaken here; it means nothing to doubt whether I am in pain!' (PI §288). But if my pain is a private object, then I *could* be mistaken, just as I could be mistaken about some public object. If I cannot be mistaken in my sincere exclamation of pain, this is not because I *infallibly* recognise my pain but because I need not recognise my pain at all to express it. So 'if someone said "I don't know if what I have is a pain or something else", we would think, perhaps, that he does not know what the English word "pain" means; and we'd explain it to him' (PI §288). Whether or not he understands that explanation will be shown 'by his use of the word, in this as in other cases' (PI §288). His apparent expression of doubt about being in pain would express misunderstanding:

> That expression of doubt has no place in the language-game; but if expressions of sensation – human behaviour – are excluded, it looks as if I might then *legitimately* begin to doubt. My temptation to say that one might take a sensation for something other than what it is arises from this: if I assume the abrogation of the normal language-game with the expression of a sensation, I need a criterion of identity for the sensation; and then the possibility of error also exists. (PI §288)

Here we rejoin the considerations of PI §270. The view that treats sensations as private objects and requires us to (re)identify them in order to name them opens the door to errors of *mis*identification. This is a corollary of the thought that my colour-impressions might differ undetectably from yours because if the application of colour-terms does not require us to have the same or similar colour-impressions, then it does not matter *what* impressions we have, and the same is true mutatis mutandis for sensations. *That* is why the hypothesis that I am mistaken when I write 'S' in my blood-pressure log is mere show if I have correlated my use of the sensation-term with increases in my blood-pressure.

13 The Beetle

The cases of the child-genius and the private diarist discourage thinking that anything has been accomplished when we try to imagine a (super)private ostensive definition of a sensation-term. If it seems that such a procedure can work, then that comes from accepting a dubious analogy between sensations and physical objects, an analogy reinforced by the misleading analogy between phenomenal and physical space. If we think of sensations as private inner objects, then we will further interpose a moment of recognition or identification between the occurrence of a sensation and its bodily or linguistic expression. However, the case of the human manometer discourages thinking that any such moment of recognition or identification occurs. This does not mean that we cannot say what sensations we have. If sensations are not superprivate objects, then we may plausibly say that they are expressed without any intermediate step, and even if sensations *were* superprivate objects, then by the private speaker's own lights their recognition would play no role in their expression because it would matter nothing for the meanings of sensation-terms what those superprivate objects were, even from one occasion to the next.

The manometer-example thus has affinities with the example of the beetle in a box (PI §293).[110] However, one task of PI §293 is to undermine the idea that I know what pain is 'only from my own case' – a goal not explicit in PI §270. Moreover, the beetle-example challenges the idea that a private object might play no role in the *use* of a sensation-term and, yet, somehow, still contribute to its *meaning*.

The passage begins with the thought (see PI §283) that I learn the meanings of sensations terms 'from my own case' (PI §293) and then combines this idea with the assumption that these sensation-terms have a use in a shared language. The conclusion is that if the word 'pain' belongs to a shared language, it does *not* get its meaning from private ostensive definition, and the temptation to think otherwise comes from objectifying sensations.

> If I say of myself that it is only from my own case that I know what the word 'pain' means – must I not say *that* of other people too? And how can I generalize the *one* case so irresponsibly?

---

[110] See, e.g., Malcolm 1954, 556; Garver 1960, 396n23; Kultgen 1968, 38; Hopkins 1974, 138–139; Senchuk 1976, 237–238; Bloor 1983, 62; Johnston 1993, 22; Diamond 2000, 275–276; Nielsen 2008, 168.

> Well, everyone tells me that he knows what pain is only from his own case! – Suppose that everyone had a box with something in it which we call a 'beetle'. No one can ever look into anyone else's box, and everyone says he knows what a beetle is only by looking at *his* beetle. – Here it would be quite possible for everyone to have something different in his box. One might even imagine such a thing constantly changing. – But what if these people's word 'beetle' had a use nonetheless? – If so, it would not be as the name of a thing. The thing in the box doesn't belong to the language-game at all; not even as a *Something*: for the box might even be empty. – No, one can 'divide through' by the thing in the box; it cancels out, whatever it is.
> That is to say, if we construe the grammar of the expression of sensation on the model of 'object and name', the object drops out of consideration as irrelevant. (PI §293)

Because sensations are *not* irrelevant to the meanings of sensation-terms,[111] we should not liken sensations to objects.

However, this passage also feeds the behaviourist worries of commentators who misinterpret the last lines. Like the manometer example, the case of the beetle inspired the misconception that Wittgenstein, while denying a role for superprivate sensations in our sensation-talk, nonetheless allows that we *have* such superprivate sensations. Thus, Pitcher remarked that Wittgenstein 'only wants to reject the idea that ... when you use the word "pain," you are referring to your sensation and telling other people that you have it' (1964, 299).[112] The idea is foreshadowed by Strawson's remark that Wittgenstein falsely believed that 'one cannot recognise or identify sensations' (1954, 86) and that, therefore, '"pain" is not the name of a sensation' (88).[113]

One variation says that Wittgenstein views sensations on the model of the inverted spectrum. You and I might have radically different experiences when we are in pain; however, 'What is irrelevant is not the existence of the object, but what it happens to be' (Donagan 1966, 347).[114] Another says that Wittgenstein takes sensation-terms to have a dual meaning: a public meaning shared by co-linguists and a private meaning or reference, knowable only to individual speakers.[115]

None of these variations is likely. The inverted spectrum, we saw, severs attributions of colour-experiences to others from the behavioural criteria for their usual attribution, and the idea that sensation-terms might have two components – a public one and a private one – is raised and criticised at PI §§273–279.

---

[111] Heil (2013, 52–54) seems to miss this step.
[112] Cf. Hadot 2010 [1959], 77; Braybrooke 1963, 675; Olscamp 1965, 243; Mundle 1966, 35–36.
[113] See also Findlay 1955, 176.
[114] See Gram 1971, 303–304. Cf. Schlick 1979 [1932], 333. Locke (1968, 106–108) adopts this view in *response* to the beetle.
[115] See Lyon 1968; Cornman 1968, 124.

More fundamentally, these readings take Wittgenstein to *accept* the analogy between beetles in boxes and sensations in bodies[116] and so misunderstand the final sentence of PI §293, which invites us *not* to model the grammar of sensation-terms on the grammar of object-talk. So the passage brings to the foreground what lies in the background of Wittgenstein's discussion of privacy and private language. – 'What I do deny is that we can construe the grammar of "having pain" by hypostatising a private object' (NPL, 451).[117]

That we should not apply the grammar of 'object and name' (PI §293) to sensation-talk was noted by many First-Wave interpreters.[118] The leading voices of the Second Wave agree,[119] and many later commentators echo this point:[120] 'A sensation is not an object' (1989, 51), says Malcolm Budd.[121] But there is disagreement on how to explicate the reasoning. On one account, their epistemic superprivacy makes private sensations irrelevant to public use[122] – we cannot *know* what others refer to when they speak of *pain*, but we can talk of pain, so the objects play no role in the meaning of this term, as they would if the object-and-name model were correct. On a related reading, the fact that the public use of 'pain' can be taught and learned without reference to superprivate pain renders the object-and-name model irrelevant.[123] The reason that the private object can play no role in the meaning of 'pain' derives from the diary-example, says Hacker: '["pain"] would not be used as the name of a thing; it would not be used as we use names for ordinary objects' (Hacker 2019b [1990], 104) because '[t]here is no *method* of comparing a sample with a private object' (2019b [1990], 104).[124] Like Hacker, Stern (2007, 266) thinks that PI §§257–258 provide the reason that the private object plays no role in the use of 'pain'. However, he thinks the objection is simply that 'the initial ceremony' of introducing the word 'beetle' for whatever is in one's box

---

[116] Mundle (1966, 43–44) finds the analogy 'apt'; Hervey (1957, 79) thinks it 'goes astray'. Neither recognises it as Wittgenstein's target.

[117] Hintikka and Hintikka (1986, 250) suggest that for Wittgenstein superprivate sensations *do* play a role in the meanings of sensation-terms, but not one modelled on ostensive definition. Superprivate sensations, they contend, can be expressed (only) by way of a public correlate (267). See Donagan 1966, 347.

[118] See Malcolm 1954, 540; Linsky 1957, 290; Cook 1965, 312; Shoemaker 1966, 358; Holborow 1967, 356; Manser 1969, 173; Thornton 1969, 271.

[119] See Goldberg 1971, 90–91; Hacker 1972, 237–238; Kenny 1973, 182; Senchuk 1976, 238; Finch 1977, 132–133.

[120] Sauvé (1985, 28–29n16) views the beetle example as a *reductio* of the supposition that I know the meaning of the word 'pain' 'only from my own case' (PI §293) but neglects the remark about grammar. Ayer (1986, 79–80), noting the remark, complains that Wittgenstein *fails* to clarify the grammar of sensation-terms.

[121] See Horwich 2012, 201. [122] See Johnston 1993, 21–22; Schroeder 2006, 208.

[123] See Williams 1983, 77; Hanfling 1989, 94; Brenner 1999, 93–94; Nielsen 2008, 167.

[124] See Glock 1996, 313. Baker (2004, 114) doubts the role of samples in the argument.

'is entirely unconnected with the rest of our language ...' (2007, 266), not that such inner ostensive definition has been shown *impossible*.

Like Stern, I think that we should not expect an attempted refutation of the possibility of private language in the *Investigations*. Like both Stern and Hacker, I think that the reason that the private object is irrelevant to the meaning of 'pain' derives from the failure of private ostensive definition. Our merely being unable to *know* what others refer to when they speak of (superprivate) *pain*, would be compatible with claiming a convergence in the shared, public use of this word, and the contention that this use could be taught and learned without the existence of superprivate pain might be thought to beg the question. By contrast, if the child-genius and the aspiring private diarist fail to define sensation-terms by inner ostensive definition, then superprivate pain does not matter for the meaning of 'pain'.

Some readers, nonetheless, interpret the beetle-example as evidence of Wittgenstein's 'Linguistic Behaviourism' (Mundle 1966, 35).[125] The temptation is reinforced – it is ironic – by the fact that in nearby passages the worry about behaviourism is, at first, lurking ...

> 'Right; but there is a Something there all the same, which accompanies my cry of pain! And it is on account of this that I utter it. And this Something is what is important – and frightful.' (PI §296)

... and then explicitly raised by one or more interlocutory voice:

> 'But you will surely admit that there is a difference between pain-behaviour with pain and pain-behaviour without pain.' – Admit it? What greater difference could there be? – 'And yet you again and again reach the conclusion that the sensation itself is a Nothing.' (PI §304)
>
> 'But you surely can't deny that, for example, in remembering, an inner process takes place.' (PI §305)
>
> To deny the mental process would mean to deny the remembering; to deny that anyone ever remembers anything. (PI §306)
>
> 'Aren't you nevertheless a behaviourist in disguise? Aren't you nevertheless basically saying that everything except human behaviour is a fiction?' (PI §307)

The responses to these worries, however, reaffirm the grammatical conclusion of the beetle-example: '– If I speak of a fiction, then it is of a *grammatical* fiction' (PI §307): namely, that sensations are to be *modelled* on physical objects or processes that involve them. Their *reality* is never in doubt.

---

[125] See Churchland 2013, 91–93.

'[Y]ou again and again reach the conclusion that the sensation itself is a Nothing.' – Not at all. It's not a Something, but not a Nothing either! The conclusion was only that a Nothing would render the same service as a Something about which nothing could be said. We've only rejected the grammar which tends to force itself on us here. (PI §304)

PI §244 suggested that we see sensation-terms like 'pain' as extensions of natural expressions of those sensations, rather than as dispassionate descriptions, based on observation, of our inner states or processes. Some such alternative is needed to produce the 'radical break' required to eliminate the 'paradox' (PI §304) of saying that a sensation is neither a something nor a nothing.

John McDowell recognises Wittgenstein's caution about the analogy between objects and sensations (1989, 292–293), but he worries that 'letting the sensation as particular drop out of consideration as irrelevant' (290n10) is 'overkill'.[126] McDowell thinks that the relevant disanalogy between sensations and ordinary objects is not that sensations are not particulars (as objects are) but that external objects 'are there for one's thinking anyway, independently of what one thinks about them' (1989, 293), whereas sensations are not. This claim is supported, he thinks, by Wittgenstein's contrast between 'describ[ing] my state of mind' and 'describ[ing] my room' (PI §290). When I *describe* my sensations (rather than merely *express* them), it is still not as though I were dispassionately observing independent objects in a private room (PI §398) or in 'a kind of peep-show box that everyone carries around in front of himself' (BT 463).

> What we call '*descriptions*' are instruments for particular uses. Think of a machine-drawing, a cross-section, an elevation with measurements, which an engineer has before him. Thinking of a description as a word-picture of the facts has something misleading about it: one tends to think only of such pictures as hang on our walls, which seem simply to depict how a thing looks, what it is like. (These pictures are, as it were, idle.) (PI §291)

When dealing with descriptions, thinks McDowell, it is legitimate to speak of objects, provided we remember that describing my sensations is very different from describing my office furniture: 'the correct point is not that sensations are not objects of reference, but that they are not objects of reference in the way external objects are' (McDowell 1989, 293).

McDowell's expression 'objects of reference' muddies the waters. Wittgenstein does not deny that we can *name* our sensations. This makes

---

[126] Cf. Hunter (1985, 105). Rorty (1980, 109–112) agrees but diagnoses Wittgenstein as conflating privileged access, which Rorty equates with first-person authority (109–110), with *qualia*. This seems wrong to me (see Section 6.2).

them 'objects of reference', but, by the same token, numbers and colours are objects of reference, and it clarifies nothing to say that naming, or referring to, or describing a colour is 'a limiting case of bringing an object under a concept' (McDowell 1989, 292) as McDowell says of sensation-talk. 'If we say, "Every word in the language signifies something", we have so far said nothing *whatever* ...' (PI §13). As we have seen (Sections 3 and 6.1), Wittgenstein encourages us to see the grammar of sensation-terms as more like the grammar of colour-words than like the grammar of names for particulars. So, although McDowell has identified *one* way in which sensations differ from spatio-temporal objects, he ignores the more general critique of the misleading analogy between physical and phenomenal space that underlies Wittgenstein's discussion of private language.[127]

Other passages on behaviourism explore the implications of treating sensations as objects. If physical objects undergo physical processes, it seems that private mental objects undergo private mental processes. Since a process is something that happens, it seems preposterous to deny such processes: surely, when I feel pain or see red, something happens!

> – The impression that we wanted to deny something arises from our setting our face against the picture of an 'inner process'. What we deny is that the picture of an inner process gives us the correct idea of the use of the word 'remember'. Indeed, we're saying that this picture, with its ramifications, stands in the way of our seeing the use of the word as it is. (PI §305)

Remembering is not a sensation. Wittgenstein is drawing connections between his treatment of sensation and perception and his treatment of other 'verbs of experience' (RPP I §836). However, the 'picture of the "inner process"' derives from the view that sensations are objects in phenomenal space – objects involved in processes and events like physical processes and events, involving familiar physical objects.

> How does the philosophical problem about mental processes and states and about behaviourism arise? – The first step is the one that altogether escapes notice. We talk of processes and states, and leave their nature undecided. Sometimes perhaps we'll know more about them – we think. But that's just what commits us to a particular way of looking at the matter. For we have a certain conception of what it means to learn to know a process better. (The decisive movement in the conjuring trick has been made, and it was the very one that seemed to us quite innocent.) – And now the analogy which was to

---

[127] McDowell reads Wittgenstein as rejecting the dualism of conceptual scheme and 'pre-conceptual given', conceding that this interpretation 'leaves some of what [Wittgenstein] says unexplained, and some looking positively mistaken' (1989, 286). In short, this reading subordinates Wittgenstein's concerns to McDowell's, even if the two make contact (e.g., at PI §261).

make us understand our thoughts falls to pieces. So we have to deny the yet uncomprehended process in the yet unexplored medium. And now it looks as if we had denied mental processes. And naturally we don't want to deny them. (PI §308)

We don't want to deny them because we don't want to deny that something happens when we think or feel pain or see red – we certainly don't want to deny that we have these experiences. But our conception of what it is to know a process better derives from our investigation of physical processes, and this is a useful model only if there are private objects in phenomenal space. That point is difficult to keep sight of, and we easily return to a picture of experience that is framed by a 'grammatical fiction'.

Worries about Wittgenstein's alleged behaviourism are further reinforced by the thought that 'someone who had *never* felt pain' could not 'understand the word "pain"' or 'could not imagine pain without having sometime felt it' (PI §315). But here we have only questions: '[H]ow do we know? How can it be decided whether it's true?' (PI §315). There is no large population of people who have never experienced pain, whom we can poll or test on the matter. But many people have never experienced colours, and it seems mistaken to say that they have *no* concept of colour, even if they can make no empirical discriminations. Someone completely blind can still learn, for example, that red light vibrates at a lower frequency than blue light, much as we all can learn that microwaves vibrate at a lower frequency than radio waves. Such a person is like someone who, according to Wittgenstein, 'may understand [the] explanation [of a game] but not be able to learn the game' (LW II 75). So the inclination to insist that the eternally unsuffering cannot know the meaning of 'pain' is a *requirement* that we impose, not a discovery that we make.

Many of the remaining passages in Wittgenstein's discussion of privacy approach this grammatical fiction from different angles. 'I know what "pain" means only from my own case' is neither an empirical proposition nor a grammatical one but 'a picture [*ein Bild*]', analogous to an 'allegorical painting' (PI §295) – like the image of justice wearing a blindfold. It holds us 'captive' (PI §115) but 'is not informative' (PI §298). It expresses only what we find ourselves 'tempted to say', which is 'not philosophy; but ... its raw material' (PI §254):

> Being unable – when we indulge in philosophical thought – to help saying something or other, being irresistibly inclined to say it – does not mean being forced into an *assumption*, or having an immediate insight into, or knowledge of, a state of affairs. (PI §299)

The sources of our temptation to say such things may be many, but especially important is our lacking '*an overview* of the use of our words' (PI §122).

So the object-and-name model is no *discovery* of philosophical inquiry but a prejudice that structures it, a 'requirement' (PI §107), given 'certain analogies between the forms of expression in different regions of our language' (PI §90). The conclusion is not that words like 'pain' are not names of sensations but that sensations do not get their names as spatio-temporal objects do. To reject 'the grammar which tends to force itself on us here' (PI §304) is not to reject the plain fact that we have sensations. The sensation is 'not a *something*' – an object that, perforce, would be superprivate, 'but not a *nothing* either!' – not a mere fiction.

14 Epilogue

I lack the space to account for *every* line of PI §§243–315, but the reading I have presented preserves the coherence and philosophical interest of these passages while respecting Wittgenstein's admonitions about philosophical problems and the practice of philosophy. Our attraction to the object-and-name model of sensation and perception is driven by the misleading analogy between phenomenal space and physical space, together with an oversimplified picture of naming. Wittgenstein's critique of these notions, beginning in 1929, is thus of central importance for understanding his critique of privacy and private language in the *Philosophical Investigations*.[128]

---

[128] I am grateful to two anonymous reviewers for extensive, helpful comments and to David Stern, Steven Burns, Thiago Dória, Gordon McOuat, Lynette Reid and audiences at the Dalhousie Philosophy Colloquium and the Atlantic Region Philosophers' Association.

Abbreviations of the Works Cited

BBB	Wittgenstein, L. (1958). *The Blue and the Brown Books*. New York: Harper Torchbooks.
BT	Wittgenstein, L. (2005). *The Big Typescript TS 213*. C. G. Luckhardt and M. A. E. Aue, trans. Oxford: Blackwell.
DS	Wittgenstein, L. (2003). 'Dictation for Schlick'. In *The Voices of Wittgenstein*. G. P. Baker, ed. London: Routledge, 1–83.
LPE	Wittgenstein, L. (1993a). 'Notes for Lectures on "Private Experience" and "Sense Data"'. D. G. Stern, ed. In *Philosophical Occasions: 1912–1951*. J. Klagge and A. Nordmann, eds. Indianapolis: Hackett, 200–288.
LW I	Wittgenstein, L. (1982). *Last Writings on the Philosophy of Psychology*, Volume I. G. H. von Wright and H. Nyman, eds., C. G. Luckhardt and M. A. E. Aue, trans. Oxford: Blackwell.
LW II	Wittgenstein, L. (1992). *Last Writings on the Philosophy of Psychology*, Volume II. G. H. von Wright and H. Nyman, eds., C. G. Luckhardt and M. A. E. Aue, trans. Oxford: Blackwell.
LWL	Wittgenstein, L. (1980a). *Wittgenstein's Lectures: Cambridge, 1930–1932*. D. Lee, ed. Chicago: University of Chicago Press.
MS	Wittgenstein, L. (1998). *Wittgensteins Nachlass. The Bergen Electronic Edition*. Oxford: Oxford University Press.
NPL	Wittgenstein, L. (1993b). 'Notes for the "Philosophical Lecture"'. D. G. Stern, ed. In *Philosophical Occasions: 1912–1951*. J. Klagge and A. Nordmann, eds. Indianapolis: Hackett, 445–458.
OC	Wittgenstein, L. (1972). *On Certainty*. G. E. M. Anscombe and G. H. von Wright, eds., D. Paul and G. E. M. Anscombe, trans. New York: Harper.
PI	Wittgenstein, L. (2009 [1968]). *Philosophical Investigations*. Rev. 4th ed., G. E. M. Anscombe, P. M. S. Hacker and J. Schulte, trans., P. M. S. Hacker and J. Schulte, eds. 3rd ed., G. E. M. Anscombe and R. Rhees, eds., G. E. M. Anscombe, trans. Oxford: Wiley-Blackwell.
PPF	Wittgenstein, L. (2009). 'Philosophy of Psychology – A Fragment'. In *Philosophical Investigations*. Revised 4th ed. P. M. S. Hacker and J. Schulte, eds. G. E. M. Anscombe, P. M. S. Hacker and J. Schulte, trans. Oxford: Wiley-Blackwell, 182–243.

PR	Wittgenstein, L. (1975). *Philosophical Remarks*. R. Rhees, ed., R. Hargreaves and R. White, trans. Chicago: University of Chicago Press.
RLF	Wittgenstein, L. (1993c). 'Some Remarks on Logical Form'. In *Philosophical Occasions: 1912–1951*. J. Klagge and A. Nordmann, eds. Indianapolis: Hackett, 29–35.
RPP I	Wittgenstein, L. (1980b). *Remarks on the Philosophy of Psychology, Vol 1*. G. E. M. Anscombe and G. H. von Wright, eds., G. E. M. Anscombe, trans. Oxford: Basil Blackwell.
RPP II	Wittgenstein, L. (1980c). *Remarks on the Philosophy of Psychology, Vol 2*. G. H. von Wright and H. Nyman, eds., C. G. Luckhardt and M. A. E. Aue, trans. Oxford: Basil Blackwell.
RSD	Wittgenstein, L. (1993d). (Rhees, R.) 'The Language of Sense Data and Private Experience'. In *Philosophical Occasions: 1912–1951*. J. Klagge and A. Nordmann, eds. Indianapolis: Hackett, 289–367.
TLP	Wittgenstein, L. (1922). *Tractatus Logico-Philosophicus*. C. K. Ogden and F. P. Ramsey, trans. London: Routledge and Kegan Paul.

References

Ambrose, A. (1954). 'Review of *Philosophical Investigations*'. *Philosophy and Phenomenological Research* 15 (1), 111–115.

Armstrong, B. (1984). 'Wittgenstein on Private Languages: It Takes Two to Talk.' *Philosophical Investigations* 7 (1), 46–62.

Ayer, A. J. (1954). 'Can There Be a Private Language?' *Proceedings of the Aristotelian Society*, Supplementary Volume 28, 63–76.

Ayer, A. J. (1973). *The Central Questions of Philosophy*. London: Weidenfeld & Nicolson.

Ayer, A. J. (1986). *Wittgenstein*. Chicago, IL: University of Chicago Press.

Baker, G. P. (1974). 'Criteria: A New Foundation for Semantics'. *Ratio* 16 (2), 156–189.

Baker, G. P. (2004). *Wittgenstein's Method: Neglected Aspects*. Oxford: Blackwell.

Baker, G. P. and P. M. S. Hacker. (1984). *Scepticism, Rules and Language*. Oxford: Blackwell.

Baker, G. P. and P. M. S. Hacker. (2005 [1983]). *Wittgenstein: Understanding and Meaning*. Part I: Essays. Oxford: Wiley Blackwell.

Baker, G. P. and P. M. S. Hacker. (2014 [1985]). *Wittgenstein: Rules, Grammar and Necessity*. Oxford: Wiley Blackwell.

Bar-on, D. (2004). *Speaking My Mind: Expression and Self-Knowledge*. Oxford: Oxford University Press.

Berger, H. (1971). 'Die soziale Struktur der Erfahrungssprache'. *Neue Hefte für Philosophie* 1, 84–107.

Blackburn, S. (1984). *Spreading the Word*. Oxford: Clarendon Press.

Bloor, D. (1983). *Wittgenstein: A Social Theory of Knowledge*. New York: Columbia University Press.

Bloor, D. (1997). *Wittgenstein, Rules and Institutions*. London: Routledge.

Bouveresse, J. (1987 [1976]). *Le mythe de l'interiorité*. Paris: Les Éditions de Minuit.

Braaten, J. (2002). 'The Short Life of Meaning: Feminism and Non-literalism'. In N. Scheman and P. O'Connor, eds., *Feminist interpretations of Ludwig Wittgenstein*. University Park, PA: Penn State University Press, 176–192.

Braybrooke, D. (1963). 'Personal Beliefs without Private Languages'. *The Review of Metaphysics* 16 (4), 672–686.

Brenner, W. H. (1999). *Wittgenstein's* Philosophical Investigations. Albany, NY: SUNY Press.

Budd, M. (1989). *Wittgenstein's Philosophy of Psychology*. London: Routledge.
Burns, S. A. M. (1994). 'If a Lion Could Talk'. *Wittgenstein Studien* 1 (1). http://sammelpunkt.philo.at/id/eprint/2190/.
Campbell, S. (1997). *Interpreting the Personal*. Ithaca, NY: Cornell University Press.
Candlish, S. (1980). 'The Real Private Language Argument'. *Philosophy* 55 (211), 85–94.
Candlish, S. (2011 [1998]). 'Wittgensteins Privatsprachenargumentation'. J. Schulte trans. In E. Von Savigny, ed., *Ludwig Wittgenstein: Philosophische Untersuchungen*. 2nd ed. Berlin: Akademie Verlag, 111–128.
Candlish, S. and G. Wrisley. (2019). 'Private Language'. *The Stanford Encyclopedia of Philosophy*. https://plato.stanford.edu/entries/private-language/ (accessed 18 January 2022).
Canfield, J. V. (1981). *Wittgenstein, Language and World*. Amherst: University of Massachusetts Press.
Canfield, J. V. (1991). 'Private Language: *Philosophical Investigations* Section 258 and Environs'. In R. Arrington and H.-J. Glock, eds., *Wittgenstein's* Philosophical Investigations: *Text and Context*. London: Routledge, 120–137.
Canfield, J. V. (1996). 'The Community View'. *The Philosophical Review* 105 (4), 469–488.
Canfield, J. V. (2001). 'Private Language: The Diary Case'. *Australasian Journal of Philosophy* 79 (3), 377–394.
Carney, J. (1960). 'Private Language: The Logic of Wittgenstein's Argument'. *Mind* 69 (276), 560–565.
Castañeda, H.-N. (1962). 'The Private-Language Argument'. In C. D. Rollins, ed., *Knowledge and Experience: Proceedings of the Third Oberlin Colloquium in Philosophy*. Pittsburgh, PA: Pittsburgh University Press, 88–105.
Cavell, S. (1969). *Must We Mean What We Say?* Cambridge: Cambridge University Press.
Cavell, S. (1979). *The Claim of Reason*. Oxford: Oxford University Press.
Churchland, P. M. (2013). *Matter and Consciousness*, 3rd ed. Cambridge, MA: MIT Press.
Clegg, J. S. (1974). 'Wittgenstein on Verification and Private Language'. *Canadian Journal of Philosophy* Supplementary Volume 1, Part 2, 205–213.
Connelly, J. (2013). 'Wittgenstein, Non-Factualism, and Deflationism'. *International Journal of Philosophical Studies* 21 (4), 559–585.
Cook, J. W. (1965). 'Wittgenstein on Privacy'. *The Philosophical Review* 74 (3), 281–314.

References

Cook, J. W. (1972). 'Solipsism and Language'. In A. Ambrose and M. Lazerowitz, eds., *Ludwig Wittgenstein: Philosophy and Language*. London: George Allen & Unwin, 37–72.

Cook, J. W. (1994). *Wittgenstein's Metaphysics*. Cambridge: Cambridge University Press.

Cooke, V. M. (1974). 'Wittgenstein's Use of the Private Language Discussion'. *International Philosophical Quarterly* 14 (1), 25–49.

Cornman, J. (1968). 'Private Languages and Private Entities'. *Australasian Journal of Philosophy* 46 (2), 117–126.

Cusmariu, A. (2022). 'The Private Language Argument: Another Footnote to Plato?' *Symposion* 9 (2), 191–222.

Dancy, J. (1985). *Introduction to Contemporary Epistemology*. Oxford: Basil Blackwell.

Davidson, D. (1984). 'First Person Authority'. *Dialectica* 38 (2–3), 101–111.

Diamond, C. (2000). 'Does Bismarck Have a Beetle in His Box?' In A. Crary and R. Read, eds., *The New Wittgenstein*. London: Routledge, 262–292.

Donagan, A. (1966). 'Wittgenstein on Sensation'. In G. Pitcher, ed., *Wittgenstein: The Philosophical Investigations*. Garden City, NY: Doubleday Anchor, 324–351.

Dummett, M. A. E. (1993a). *Origins of Analytical Philosophy*. London: Duckworth.

Dummett, M. A. E. (1993b). *The Seas of Language*. Oxford: Clarendon.

Dunlop, C. (1984). 'Wittgenstein on Sensation and "Seeing-As"'. *Synthese* 60 (3), 349–367.

Emmons, D. C. (1968). 'Two Dialogues'. *Dialogue* 7, 410–429.

Fan, Z. (2021). 'A Critical Discussion of the "Memory-Challenge" to Interpretations of the Private Language Argument'. *Journal for the History of Analytical Philosophy* 9 (4), 47–58.

Finch, H. L. (1977). *Wittgenstein – The Later Philosophy*. Atlantic Highlands, NJ: Humanities Press.

Findlay, J. N. (1955). Review of *Philosophical Investigations*. *Philosophy* 30 (113), 173–179.

Fogelin, R. J. (1976). *Wittgenstein*, 1st ed. London: Routledge.

Fogelin, R. J. (1987). *Wittgenstein*, 2nd ed. London: Routledge.

Fogelin, R. J. (1994). *Pyrrhonian Reflections on Knowledge and Justification*. Oxford: Oxford University Press.

Fogelin, R. J. (2009). *Taking Wittgenstein at His Word: A Textual Study*. Princeton: Princeton University Press.

Garver, N. (1960). 'Wittgenstein on Private Language'. *Philosophy and Phenomenological Research* 20 (3), 389–396.

Geach, P. (1957). *Mental Acts*. London: Routledge & Kegan Paul.

Gert, B. (1986). 'Wittgenstein's Private Language Arguments'. *Synthese* 68 (3), 409–439.

Gert, H. (2000). 'Review: Recent Books on Wittgenstein'. *The Philosophical Quarterly* 50 (198), 98–104.

Glock, H.-J. (1996). *A Wittgenstein Dictionary*. Oxford: Blackwell.

Goldberg, B. (1971). 'The Linguistic Expression of Feeling'. *American Philosophical Quarterly* 8 (1), 86–92.

Gram, M. (1971). 'Privacy and Language'. In E. D. Klemke, ed., *Essays on Wittgenstein*. Chicago, IL: University of Illinois Press, 298–327.

Grayling, A. C. (1988). *Wittgenstein*. Oxford: Oxford University Press.

Gruender, C. D. (1968). 'Language, Society, and Knowledge'. *The Antioch Review* 28 (2), 187–212.

Hacker, P. M. S. (1972). *Insight and Illusion: Wittgenstein on Philosophy and the Metaphysics of Experience*. Oxford: Clarendon.

Hacker, P. M. S. (2019a [1990]). *Wittgenstein Meaning and Mind*, Part I Essays. 2nd ed. Oxford: Blackwell.

Hacker, P. M. S. (2019b [1990]). *Wittgenstein Meaning and Mind*, Part II Exegesis §§243–427. 2nd ed. Oxford: Blackwell.

Hadot, P. (2010 [1959]). 'Wittgenstein philosophe du langage II'. In *Wittgenstein et les limites du langage*. Paris: J. Vrin, 67–82.

Hallett, G. (1977). *A Companion to Wittgenstein's 'Philosophical Investigations'*. Ithaca, NY: Cornell University Press.

Hanfling, O. (1984). 'What Does the Private Language Argument Prove?' *The Philosophical Quarterly* 34 (137), 468–481.

Hanfling, O. (1989). *Wittgenstein's Later Philosophy*. Albany, NY: SUNY Press.

Haque, A. (1984). 'The Concept of Private Language'. *Darshan-Manjari: The Burdwan University Journal of Philosophy* 1, 32–39.

Hardin, C. L. (1959). 'Wittgenstein on Private Languages'. *The Journal of Philosophy* 56 (12), 517–528.

Hartnack, J. (1965). *Wittgenstein and Modern Philosophy*. M. Cranston trans. New York: Anchor Books.

Heath, P. L. (1956). 'Wittgenstein Investigated'. *The Philosophical Quarterly* 6 (22), 66–71.

Heil, J. (2013). *Philosophy of Mind: A Contemporary Introduction*. 3d ed. New York: Routledge.

Hertzberg, L. (2023). *Wittgenstein on Criteria and Practices*. Cambridge: Cambridge University Press.

Hervey, H. (1957). 'The Private Language Problem'. *The Philosophical Quarterly* 7 (26), 63–79.

Hintikka, J. (1969). 'Wittgenstein on Private Language: Some Sources of Misunderstanding'. *Mind* 78 (311), 423–425.

Hintikka, J. and M. B. Hintikka (1986). *Investigating Wittgenstein*. Oxford: Blackwell.

Hodges, M. (1976). 'Nominalism and the Private Language Argument'. *The Southern Journal of Philosophy* 14 (3), 283–291.

Holborow, L. C. (1967). 'Wittgenstein's Kind of Behaviourism?' *The Philosophical Quarterly* 17 (69), 345–357.

Hopkins, J. (1974). 'Wittgenstein and Physicalism'. *Proceedings of the Aristotelian Society* 75, 121–146.

Horwich, P. (2012). *Wittgenstein's Metaphilosophy*. Oxford: Oxford University Press.

Hunter, J. F. M. (1985). *Understanding Wittgenstein*. Edinburgh: Edinburgh University Press.

Hymers, M. (1997). 'Kant's Private-Clock Argument'. *Kant-Studien* 88, 442–461.

Hymers, M. (2010). *Wittgenstein and the Practice of Philosophy*. Peterborough: Broadview.

Hymers, M. (2017). *Wittgenstein on Sensation and Perception*. New York: Routledge.

Hymers, M. (2021). 'Wittgenstein on Aspect-Recognition in Philosophy and Mathematics'. *Philosophical Investigations* 44 (1), 71–98.

Jacobsen, R. (1996). 'Wittgenstein on Self-Knowledge and Self-Expression'. *The Philosophical Quarterly* 46 (182), 12–30.

Jacobsen, R. (1997). 'Semantic Character and Expressive Content'. *Philosophical Papers* 26 (2), 129–146.

Jacquette, D. (1997). *Wittgenstein's Thought in Transition*. West Lafayette, IN: Purdue University Press.

Johnston, P. (1993). *Wittgenstein: Rethinking the Inner*. London: Routledge.

Kanterian, E. (2017). 'Privacy and Private Language'. In H.-J. Glock and J. Hyman, eds., *A Companion to Wittgenstein*. Oxford: Wiley, 445–464.

Kenny, A. (1966). 'Cartesian Privacy'. In G. Pitcher, ed., *Wittgenstein: The Philosophical Investigations*. New York: Doubleday, 352–370.

Kenny, A. (1973). *Wittgenstein*. London: Pelican Books.

Kienzler, W. (2007). *Ludwig Wittgensteins 'Philosophische Untersuchungen'*. Darmstadt: Wissenschaftliche Buchgesellschaft.

Kimball, R. (1980). 'Private Criteria and the Private Language Argument'. *The Southern Journal of Philosophy* 18 (4), 411–416.

Klagge, J. (2016). *Simply Wittgenstein*. New York: Simply Charly.

Klein, P. (1969). 'The Private Language Argument and the Sense-Datum Theory'. *Australasian Journal of Philosophy* 47 (3), 325–343.

Koethe, J. (1996). *The Continuity of Wittgenstein's Thought*. Ithaca, NY: Cornell University Press.

Kripke, S. (1982). *Wittgenstein on Rules and Private Language*. Cambridge, MA: Harvard University Press.

Kultgen, J. H. (1968). 'Can There Be a Public Language?' *The Southern Journal of Philosophy* 6 (1), 31–44.

Kusch, M. (2006). *A Sceptical Guide to Meaning and Rules: Defending Kripke's Wittgenstein*. Montreal: McGill-Queen's University Press.

Law, S. (2004). 'Five Private Language Arguments'. *International Journal of Philosophical Studies* 12 (2), 159–176.

Levin, M. (1973). 'Wittgenstein in Perspective'. *Social Research* 40 (1), 192–207.

Lin, F. Y. (2017). 'Wittgenstein's Private Language Investigation'. *Philosophical Investigations* 40 (3), 257–281.

Lin, F. Y. (2021). 'The "Grammatical" Nature of Wittgenstein's Private Language Investigation'. *Philosophical Forum* 52, 139–163.

Linsky, L. (1957). 'Wittgenstein on Language and Some Problems of Philosophy'. *The Journal of Philosophy* 54 (10), 285–293.

Locke, D. (1968). *Myself and Others*. London: Oxford University Press.

Lycan, W. G. (1971). 'Noninductive Evidence: Recent Work on Wittgenstein's "Criteria"'. *American Philosophical Quarterly* 8 (2): 109–125.

Lyon, A. (1968). 'Family Resemblance, Vagueness, and Change of Meaning'. *Theoria: A Swedish Journal of Philosophy* 34, 66–75.

Madell, G. (2018). 'Last Rites for the Private Language Argument'. *Philosophy* 93, 53–67.

Malcolm, N. (1954). 'Wittgenstein's *Philosophical Investigations*'. *The Philosophical Review* 63 (4), 530–559.

Malcolm, N. (1967). 'The Privacy of Experience'. In A. Stroll, ed., *Epistemology: New Essays in the Theory of Knowledge*. New York: Harper and Row, 129–158.

Malcolm, N. (1977). *Thought and Knowledge*. Ithaca, NY: Cornell University Press.

Malcolm, N. (1989). 'Wittgenstein on Language and Rules'. *Philosophy* 64, 5–28.

Manser, A. (1969). 'Pain and Private Language'. In P. Winch, ed., *Studies in the Philosophy of Wittgenstein*. New York: Humanities Press, 166–183.

Marion, M. (2022). 'Wittgenstein, Dialectic and Pyrrhonism'. Atlantic Region Philosophers' Association. Dalhousie University, Halifax, Canada.

Marks, C. (1975). 'Verificationism, Scepticism, and the Private Language Argument'. *Philosophical Studies* 28 (3), 151–171.

Martin, R. M. (1987). *The Meaning of Language*. Cambridge, MA: MIT Press.

Martinich, A. P. and D. Sosa, eds. (2013). *The Philosophy of Language*, 6th ed. Oxford: Oxford University Press.

Maslin, K. T. (2001). *An Introduction to the Philosophy of Mind*. Cambridge: Polity Press.

McDougall, D. A. (2013). 'The Role of *Philosophical Investigations* § 258: What Is "the Private Language Argument"?' *Analytic Philosophy* 54 (1), 44–71.

McDowell, J. (1982). 'Criteria, Defeasibility and Knowledge'. *Proceedings of the British Academy* 68, 455–479.

McDowell, J. (1989). 'One Strand in the Private Language Argument'. *Grazer Philosophische Studien* 33, 285–303.

McGinn, C. (1984). *Wittgenstein on Meaning: An Interpretation and Evaluation*. Oxford: Blackwell.

McGinn, M. (2013 [1997]). *The Routledge Guidebook to Wittgenstein's* Philosophical Investigations. London: Routledge.

Medina, J. (2002). *The Unity of Wittgenstein's Philosophy*. Albany, NY: SUNY Press.

Moore, G. E. (1903). 'The Refutation of Idealism'. *Mind* n.s. 12 (48), 433–453.

Moore, G. E. (1909–10). 'The Subject-Matter of Psychology'. *Proceedings of the Aristotelian Society* n.s. 10, 36–62.

Morstein, P. von. (1980). 'Kripke, Wittgenstein, and the Private Language Argument'. *Grazer Philosophische Studien* 11, 61–74.

Mulhall, S. (2007). *Wittgenstein's Private Language: Grammar, Nonsense, and Imagination in* Philosophical Investigations, *§§243–315*. Oxford: Clarendon Press.

Mundle, C. W. K. (1966). '"Private Language" and Wittgenstein's Kind of Behaviourism'. *The Philosophical Quarterly* 16 (62), 35–46.

Neitz, J. and Gerald H. Jacobs. (1986). 'Polymorphism of the Long-wavelength Cone in Normal Human Colour Vision'. *Nature* 323, 623–625.

Nielsen, K. S. (2008). *The Evolution of the Private Language Argument*. London: Ashgate.

Olscamp, P. J. (1965). 'Wittgenstein's Refutation of Skepticism'. *Philosophy and Phenomenological Research* 26 (2), 239–247.

Papineau, D. (2011). 'Phenomenal Concepts and the Private Language Argument'. *American Philosophical Quarterly* 48 (2), 175–184.

Passmore, J. (1957). *A Hundred Years of Philosophy*. London: Duckworth.

Pastoureau, M and D. Simonet. (2014). *Le Petit livre des couleurs*. Paris: Éditions Points.

Peacocke, C. (1981). 'Rule-Following: The Nature of Wittgenstein's Arguments'. In S. H. Holtzman and C. M. Leich, eds., *Wittgenstein: To Follow a Rule*. London: Routledge & Kegan Paul, 72–95.

Pears, D. (1971). *Wittgenstein*. London: Fontana.

Pears, D. (1988). *The False Prison: A Study of the Development of Wittgenstein's Philosophy*. Volume 2. Oxford: Clarendon Press.

Pears, D. (2006). *Paradox and Platitude in Wittgenstein's Philosophy*. Oxford: Clarendon.

Perkins, M. (1965). 'Two Arguments against a Private Language'. *The Journal of Philosophy* 62 (17), 443–459.

Pitcher, G. (1964). *The Philosophy of Wittgenstein*. Englewood Cliffs, NJ: Prentice-Hall.

Pole, D. (1958). *Later Philosophy of Wittgenstein*. Fair Lawn, NJ: Essential Books.

Potter, E. (1993). 'Gender and Epistemic Negotiation'. In L. Alcoff and E. Potter, eds., *Feminist Epistemologies*. New York: Routledge, 161–186.

Price, J. T. (1973). *Language and Being in Wittgenstein's* Philosophical Investigations. The Hague: Mouton.

Putnam. H. (1994). *Words and Life*. Cambridge, MA: Harvard University Press.

Quine, W. V. O. (1969). *Ontological Relativity and Other Essays*. New York: Columbia University Press.

Ramsey, F. P. (1923). 'Critical Notice: "*Tractatus Logico-Philosophicus*, by Ludwig Wittgenstein"'. *Mind* n.s. 32 (128), 465–478.

Rembert, A. (1975). 'Wittgenstein on Learning the Names of Inner States'. *The Philosophical Review* 84 (2), 236–248.

Rhees, R. (1954). 'Can There Be a Private Language?' *Proceedings of the Aristotelian Society*, Supplementary Volume 28, 77–94.

Robinson, H. (1994). *Perception*. London: Routledge.

Rorty, R. (1980). *Philosophy and the Mirror of Nature*. Princeton, NJ: Princeton University Press.

Rundle, B. (2009). 'The Private Language Argument'. In H.-J. Glock and J. Hyman, eds., *Wittgenstein and Analytic Philosophy: Essays for P. M. S. Hacker*. Oxford: Oxford University Press, 133–151.

Ryle, G. (1949). *The Concept of Mind*. London: Hutchinson's University Library.

Saunders, J. T. and D. F. Henze (1967). *The Private-Language Problem: A Philosophical Dialogue*. New York: Random House.

Sauvé, D. (1985). 'L'argument du langage privé'. *Dialogue* 24, 3–31.

Sauvé, D. (1988). 'Le probleme du 'langage 'privé'' et la conception wittgensteinienne du langage'. *Dialogue* 27, 417–449.

Savigny, E. von. (2019 [1988]). *Wittgensteins 'philosophische Untersuchungen': Ein Kommentar für Leser*, 3rd ed. Frankfurt am Main: Klostermann.

Schlick, M. (1979 [1932]). 'Form and Content: An Introduction to Philosophical Thinking'. In H. Mulder and B. F. B. van de Velde-Schlick, eds., *Philosophical Papers*, Volume 2. Dordrecht: D. Reidel, 285–369.

Schroeder, S. (2006). *Wittgenstein: The Way Out of the Fly Bottle*. Cambridge: Polity.

Schroeder, S. (2013). 'Can I Have Your Pain?' *Philosophical Investigations* 36 (3), 201–209.

Schulte, J. (1992). *Wittgenstein: An Introduction*. W. H. Brenner and J. F. Holley trans. Albany: SUNY Press.

Schulte, J. (2011). 'Privacy'. In M. McGinn and O. Kuusela eds., *The Oxford Handbook of Wittgenstein*. Oxford: Oxford University Press, 429–450.

Senchuk, D. (1976). 'Private Objects: A Study of Wittgenstein's Method'. *Metaphilosophy* 7 (3–4), 217–240.

Shoemaker, S. (1966). Review of *The Philosophy of Wittgenstein* by George Pitcher. *The Journal of Philosophy* 63 (12), 354–358.

Sluga, H. (2011). *Wittgenstein*. Oxford: Wiley-Blackwell.

Snowdon, P. (2011). 'Private Experience and Sense-Data'. In M. McGinn and O. Kuusela eds., *The Oxford Handbook of Wittgenstein*. Oxford: Oxford University Press, 402–428.

Soames, S. (2003). *Philosophical Analysis in the Twentieth Century*, Volume 2. Princeton, NJ: Princeton University Press.

Stainton, R. J. (1996). *Philosophical Perspectives on Language*. Peterborough: Broadview,

Stern, D. G. (1994). 'A New Exposition of the "Private Language Argument": Wittgenstein's "Notes for the 'Philosophical Lecture'"'. *Philosophical Investigations* 17 (3), 552–565.

Stern, D. G. (1995). *Wittgenstein on Mind and Language*. Oxford: Oxford University Press.

Stern, D. G. (2004). *Wittgenstein's* Philosophical Investigations: *An Introduction*. Cambridge: Cambridge University Press.

Stern, D. G. (2007). 'The Uses of Wittgenstein's Beetle: *Philosophical Investigations* §293 and its Interpreters'. In G. Kahane, E. Kanterian and O. Kuusela, eds., *Wittgenstein and His Interpreters: Essays in Memory of Gordon Baker*, Oxford: Blackwell, 248–268.

Stern, K. (1963). 'Private Language and Skepticism'. *The Journal of Philosophy* 60 (24), 745–759.

Stocker, M. (1966). 'Memory and the Private Language Argument'. *The Philosophical Quarterly* 16 (62), 47–53.

Strawson, P. F. (1954). Critical Notice of *Philosophical Investigations*. *Mind* 63 (249), 70–99.

Stroud, B. (2002 [1983]). 'Wittgenstein's "Treatment" of the Quest for "A Language Which Describes My Inner Experiences and Which Only I Myself Can Understand"'. In *Meaning, Understanding, and Practice: Philosophical Essays*. Oxford: Oxford University Press, 67–79.

Szabados, B. (1981). 'Wittgenstein on "Mistrusting One's Own Belief"'. *Canadian Journal of Philosophy* 11 (4), 603–612.

Tanburn, N. P. (1963). 'Private Languages Again'. *Mind* 72 (285), 88–102.

Tanesini, A. (2004). *Wittgenstein: A Feminist Interpretation*. Cambridge: Polity.

Tang, H. (2014). 'Wittgenstein and the Dualism of the Inner and the Outer'. *Synthese* 191 (14), 3173–3194.

Tang, H. (2015). 'A Meeting of the Conceptual and the Natural: Wittgenstein on Learning a Sensation-Language'. *Philosophy and Phenomenological Research* 91 (1), 105–135.

Tanner, S. (1986). Abstract of 'The Private Language Problem'. Doctoral Dissertation. University of Illinois, Urbana-Champagne. https://philpapers.org/rec/TANTPL. Accessed 7 July 2022.

Temkin, J. (1986). 'A Private Language Argument'. *The Southern Journal of Philosophy* 24 (1), 109–121.

Thomson, J. J. (1964). 'Private Languages'. *American Philosophical Quarterly* 1 (1), 20–31.

Thornton, M. T. (1969). 'Locke's Criticism of Wittgenstein'. *The Philosophical Quarterly* 19 (76), 266–271.

Todd, W. (1962). 'Private Languages'. *The Philosophical Quarterly* 12 (48), 206–217.

Tugendhat, E. (1986). *Self-Consciousness and Self-Determination*. P. Stern, trans. Cambridge, MA: MIT Press.

Verheggen, C. (2007). 'The Community View Revisited'. *Metaphilosophy* 38 (5), 612–631.

Villanueva, E. (1972). 'Prof. Pears sobre Wittgenstein'. *Crítica: Revista Hispanoamericana de Filosofía* 6 (16/17), 131–138.

Vohra, A. (1976). 'Privacy and Private Language'. *Indian Philosophical Quarterly* 3, 505–524.

von Wright, G. H. (1993). 'The Wittgenstein Papers'. In J. Klagge and A. Nordmann, eds., *Philosophical Occasions: 1912–1951*. Indianapolis, IN: Hackett, 480–506.

Wellman, C. (1959). 'Wittgenstein and the Egocentric Predicament'. *Mind* 68 (270), 223–233.

Wellman, C. (1962). 'Wittgenstein's Conception of a Criterion'. *The Philosophical Review* 71 (4), 433–447.

Werhane, P. (1989). 'Does "Obeying a Rule Is a Practice" Imply a Community View of Language?' *Metaphilosophy* 20, 134–151.

Williams, M. (1983). 'Wittgenstein on Representation, Privileged Objects, and Private Languages'. *Canadian Journal of Philosophy* 13 (1), 57–78.

Williams, M. (1999). *Wittgenstein, Mind and Meaning: Towards a Social Conception of Mind*. London: Routledge.

Wilson, B. (1998). *Wittgenstein's Philosophical Investigations: A Guide*. Edinburgh: Edinburgh University Press.

Winch, P. (1958). *The Idea of a Social Science and Its Relation to Philosophy*. London: Routledge & Kegan Paul.

Wright, C. (1980). *Wittgenstein on the Foundations of Mathematics*. Cambridge, MA: Harvard University Press.

Wright, C. (2001). *Rails to Infinity: Essays on Themes from Wittgenstein's Philosophical Investigations*. Cambridge, MA: Harvard University Press.

Wrisley, G. (2011). 'Wherefore the Failure of Private Ostension?' *Australasian Journal of Philosophy* 89 (3), 483–498.

Ziedins, R. (1966). 'The Possibility of Scepticism about Perception'. *The Philosophical Quarterly* 16 (65), 329–340.

In memory of Steven Burns – mentor, colleague, friend.

Cambridge Elements

The Philosophy of Ludwig Wittgenstein

David G. Stern
University of Iowa
David G. Stern is a Professor of Philosophy and a Collegiate Fellow in the College of Liberal Arts and Sciences at the University of Iowa. His research interests include history of analytic philosophy, philosophy of language, philosophy of mind, and philosophy of science. He is the author of *Wittgenstein's Philosophical Investigations: An Introduction* (Cambridge University Press, 2004) and *Wittgenstein on Mind and Language* (Oxford University Press, 1995), as well as more than 50 journal articles and book chapters. He is the editor of *Wittgenstein in the 1930s: Between the 'Tractatus' and the 'Investigations'* (Cambridge University Press, 2018) and is also a co-editor of the *Cambridge Companion to Wittgenstein* (Cambridge University Press, 2nd edition, 2018), *Wittgenstein: Lectures, Cambridge 1930–1933, from the Notes of G. E. Moore* (Cambridge University Press, 2016) and *Wittgenstein Reads Weininger* (Cambridge University Press, 2004).

About the Series
This series provides concise and structured introductions to all the central topics in the philosophy of Ludwig Wittgenstein. The Elements are written by distinguished senior scholars and bright junior scholars with relevant expertise, producing balanced and comprehensive coverage of the full range of Wittgenstein's thought.

Cambridge Elements

The Philosophy of Ludwig Wittgenstein

Elements in the Series

Wittgenstein on Criteria and Practices
Lars Hertzberg

Wittgenstein on Religious Belief
Genia Schönbaumsfeld

Wittgenstein and Aesthetics
Hanne Appelqvist

Style, Method and Philosophy in Wittgenstein
Alois Pichler

Wittgenstein on Realism and Idealism
David R. Cerbone

Wittgenstein and Ethics
Anne-Marie Søndergaard Christensen

Wittgenstein and Russell
Sanford Shieh

Wittgenstein on Music
Eran Guter

Wittgenstein on Knowledge and Certainty
Danièle Moyal-Sharrock and Duncan Pritchard

Wittgenstein on Colour, 1916–1950
Andrew Lugg

Wittgenstein and Social Epistemology
Annalisa Coliva

Wittgenstein on Private Language, Sensation and Perception
Michael Hymers

A full series listing is available at: www.cambridge.org/EPLW

Printed by Integrated Books International,
United States of America